BREAKING FREE

GOOD TO GO 1

JEFFREY VONK

ISBN: 9789493056145 (ebook)

ISBN: 9789493056152 (paperback)

Publisher: Amsterdam Publishers

CONTENTS

This book is dedicated to my parents and older brother. Three people who never took the time to get to know me.

Hope this helps.

INTRODUCTION

The late Wilbur E. Garrett once wrote: "When we try to explain the daredevil behavior of a cat we say 'Curiosity killed the cat' and when it somehow survives we cover that with 'A cat has nine lives'. The same could be said about explorers."

When I ran away from home for the first time I was only three years old. It's actually my very first memory. My dad was a bricklayer but due to a back injury, he spent most of his time as a security guard at a factory, if he wasn't busy volunteering at the fire fighters, so I didn't see him often. Therefore, my mother was usually the one to take my brother and me to school on the bicycle, which is quite common in the Netherlands. Propped against the child seat in the back, I was always absorbing my surroundings with a growing urge to question the unknown, laying a foundation for intrusiveness so to speak.

Back home my mother would return to her daily chores like doing the laundry, which she takes a bit too seriously by even ironing the washcloths. During one of these unguarded, busy moments I saw a chance for my long-anticipated escape. Having crossed the traffic-filled street I vanished into forbidden terrain. Young as I was, I still recall the euphoria of nobody looking over my shoulder or correcting me. I wasn't put on this earth to live like a bird in a cage; somehow, there has always been the need to break free. Turns out the good Lord had blessed me with a photographic memory and I ended up following the same path to the elementary school my older brother went to. From my bicycle seat, I had memorized the entire route whilst figuring out a shortcut with my built-in compass. However, I was presented with a small challenge. In those days, the municipality was digging a huge canal straight through the village establishing new suburbs. Builders had left a timber beam across the still dry canal at a height of about six yards.

Step-by-step my little feet slide forward, the muddy bottom ready to gorge my tiny existence. When the timber starts to tremble, I hesitate for a second. Quickly overcoming my anxiety, I finally reach the other side. While relishing in this personal triumph my poor mother is wiping the sweat from her brow. Where can her little boy be? He's nowhere to be found. Expecting the worst, hastened feet stride to the dike to see whether I'm floating face-down in the lake, or drowned in one of the many surrounding watery trenches. Neighbors notice her state of panic and within minutes the whole block is searching along with my mother. The fear of any parent became a reality for her – her toddler was missing!

Many fretful hours pass until teachers at the elementary school notice an unfamiliar whipper-snapper contentedly minding his own business in the sandpit. Convinced of my innocence I was reunited with the home front later that day. I suppose it's fair to say that it has always been in my blood and this independent mission was the genesis of many more to come.

I am sure you have seen them, those guys with patches of flags of all the countries they have visited sewn onto their bags. Of course, backpacking is not necessarily a new thing. These days, expanding your opportunities is rather the thing to do in a world that is getting smaller and smaller – perhaps now more than ever. The popularity of backpacking has increased thanks to slick travel magazines and a surplus of flashy television programs. Also, let us not forget that due to social media, outdoor stores have seen their net revenues doubled. Ever since the number of millennials striving to visit the wonders of the world in record time, in order to fill their travel blogs and Instagram pages, it has skyrocketed. Many youngsters will usually travel as much as they can before rushing back for their master's degree for a discipline they will never get a job for. Still, the need to extricate from the mandated matrix is flourishing. Not to mention the new generation of bracelet-braiding hippies; zoned out on the sidewalks by excessive drug use, trying to make a buck selling those bracelets that were already tacky in the stone age, or playing a few cords on sticker-covered guitars, with uncut strings.

But no judgment here – to each his own. Everyone has their own path to walk. Some of us prefer to look and smell like a homeless person, which I'm not foreign to myself. It's all about letting go of the conventional to unleash that shackled inner self, but what does it really mean to visit another country and ingest an abstract language, eat unknown food and dwell in the midst of a culture with such different habits, morals and values? Surely, hanging out in hostels all day doesn't teach you much of the place.

Friends ask "How is your holiday going?" But make no mistake. To me a holiday is – relaxing or active – being surrounded by comfort and security, having your primary needs within reach. To experience the essence of traveling, or true backpacking if you will, one must think in terms of lacking those primary needs.

How about having ice cold showers for a few months? Do you know what that does to a human body or human spirit? Could you handle not having a good sponge for days on end, being dirty and having stinky clothes? Not knowing where you will sleep at night, if at all, or having to find shelter against the freezing air or a sudden downpour? Are you up for making judgment calls in an unsafe area with potential robbers watching you? In addition, you may also have to deal with a hungry pack of dogs who don't look very friendly. Sometimes, in urban or inhabited areas, you may have to hold number one and number two for hours before finding a bathroom. And once it is found... there is no paper. Furthermore, searching for a decent meal means that sometimes you may have to deal with an empty stomach for hours before finding anything edible.

How do you communicate your desires if no one understands what you're saying? Believe me, in many places locals don't even know the word for 'water' in English. Imagine that situation when you're dying of thirst the whole day. Did your colleagues who asked how the holiday was going think about travel insurance? Or how to deal with a stolen passport? Or how to act when your wallet is empty and no one has heard of an ATM, or where to arrange transport if you're on your own in a remote place? Or how to find gasoline with zero gas stations around for miles and miles, and what the hell are miles anyway when you are used to counting in kilometers? Probably the worst thing for most people is the lack of internet for a while, and by that I'm not talking about a mere couple of hours. Not being able to navigate, make travel plans online or communicate with family and friends can be difficult obstacles to overcome. Another often-neglected issue is the culture shock one experiences when going back home. How do you reintegrate into society when you were subject to such a different lifestyle, or when you simply don't have a home to return to? If you go abroad for weeks, months, or years, only one thing has significantly changed when you come back, and that is you.

Okay, now we're starting to get the hang of it. There are indeed quite a few strings attached to traveling. Having said that, it's clear that no one would go into the wild if the hardships weren't worth it. You can end up being astounded by the beauty of multi-colored mountains sitting 12,000 feet above sea level, dwell in the sheer awe of deserts as far as the eye can see or, a place teeming with wildlife that makes you feel truly one with nature – this is your deserved reward. Who can resist jaw-dropping sunrises over ancient geometrical buildings in overgrown jungles, meeting indigenous people in traditional clothing along the way? Who doesn't dream of white sandy beaches beneath a cloudless sky, indulging in warm temperatures surrounded by coconut-filled palm trees when diving in turquoise lagoons?

Traveling reveals the true meaning of the word *recreation*. If you allow me to speak for most of the others like me, that's exactly why we do it. In addition, the opportunity for experiencing personal growth is unprecedented and the knowledge you gain is a gift for the rest of your life as well as for others along the way, the enjoyment of which becomes an everlasting memory.

On more than one occasion, people have told me that I am on the run. In their minds I'm fleeing from something or at least have certain issues for all this pavement chasing. The truth, which apparently some find hard to understand, is that sometimes I just want to see a country! I have this unquenchable curiosity and undying interest in the unexplored. When I am home for too long, if such a thing exists at all, I get homesick for adventure. Is the longing to learn my drug? Maybe it is, but man do I feel alive while being on the move.

Another figurative vertebral column was strengthened in the year 1992. Having crossed several borders my family and I end up in the vicinity of charming Luxembourg. Still a boy at this point of my life I remember the fresh smells of yellow knee-high grass fields, with the brightness of the midday summer sun making our eyes pinch as I French-kiss a girl for the first time. Although this memory sticks with me as unforgettable, the next event sticks out even more.

Amidst the Ardennes, a rugged yet gorgeous mountain range, the campground where we were staying at facilitated a *nightly dropping*. Meaning they would kick us out of a van in the middle of nowhere where we sat blindfolded, only for us to find our way back to the campground again. Arguably the only adventurous thing my parents ever did, they decide to take my brother and me to join the group which existed of approximately seventy people. Once started we march for hours through dense forest, with only a dynamo torch as our source of light. The brave men walk at the front, unknowingly leading us away from our destination by many miles, and encumbered by testosterone it takes a while before they admit we are utterly lost. Take note, this is in an era well before the invention of smartphones and the like. Increasingly concerned, clammy faces stare at the road map, with many women now seemingly worried for the wellbeing of their children as exhaustion and dehydration seeps in. Just when the threatening night seems to lure us further into the wrong direction, a twelve-year-old lad addresses the men claiming to know the way. "I know exactly where we are!" he says. Being more proud than brave, the men harden their hearts and don't want anything to do with him. Contrary to feeling like a loner, or an outsider even, it has always been remarkably easy for me to connect with others. It so happened that newly-acquainted friends and I had spent a previous week and a half together continuously scouring the woods. Due to my natural tendency to memorize things, I knew every rock, every bush and every trail like the back of my hand. After a lengthy game of persuasion, they eventually follow my lead with the whole group on my tail. Whether with certainty or doubt, they still follow me, bringing an incredible smile to my face. Maybe more like a smirk.

Suddenly I had a voice, something that would never have happened had I chosen to stay at home. Now I had given them hope to make it back to their own beds and be reunited with their loved ones left behind at the campground. All those adults placing their trust into the hands of a child is a feeling I'll never forget. I will likewise never forget the look on the brave men's faces as I safely returned everyone back to civilization. Those humbled looks and proud mouths silenced, I cherish like trophies on the mantelpiece. Forevermore, priceless.

Cliché memes say that life is a book – if you don't travel you only read the first page – and in this case, I will have to agree with that.

Once, while working at a disorganized woodpile in the state of Missouri, I made some cash by dismantling old pallets. Here I asked a Chicago resident if he also liked to barbecue on the lakeside back home, since it was crowded as heck there in the summertime. He replied: "What lake?" In reality, he'd never skipped beyond that first page, therefore missing out on so much splendor. Being over thirty the good man spent his whole life in the city and had never seen Lake Michigan, despite it being right under his nose!

Another question that I often get is: "How do you finance all of this?" People have to understand that it's about priorities and sometimes sacrifices. Going to your favorite restaurant every week is not helping if you want to travel, nor is following the latest, ever-changing fashion trends. As for me, I don't drink, I don't smoke, and the biggest money saver might be the fact that as of yet I don't have kids. Also, I don't care about extravagant houses, cars and all kinds of worldly possessions. I have everything arranged pretty well for the small company I own, being a general contractor, but that's it. These are mere investments to fill the piggy bank. That proverbial piggy bank gets smashed to pieces by the first good idea that pops up to hit the road. Transforming these ideas into actually stuffing my backpack and going is unimaginable for some, yet so easy for me.

I remember seeing my parents' bedroom as a child. Weeks before the start of our summer holiday my mom would already have opened up suitcases on the floor. Accompanied by a long, handwritten checklist, filling them until they almost wouldn't close anymore. Nowadays, I gather my stuff literally an hour before I leave and as far as I know, I have never forgotten anything. Unfortunately, airline or bus companies have lost my luggage quite a few times, and while it's no fun you always find a way to manage. Ultimately, making your dreams come true is what it's all about. I hope that this book will allow you to see how my ideas and dreams became reality. Sometimes a little too close to the matter.

In a no-nonsense, unexaggerated way I tried my best to tell it as it happened. Not only do I have a very good memory but I always keep a journal to maintain track of my travels. These recollections, thoughts and emotions aren't loosely based on events, they *are* actual events that eventually turned into the fine copy you hold in your hands right now. Compare it to a logbook with infotainment. In this volume, you will be treated to stories of my time in Asia, the Middle East and a slim slice of Africa and Europe.

You may find it easy to understand why most things are still so vivid to me. Hopefully, you develop a chronic itch as I have because there is a lot of beauty out there. But even if traveling never becomes your thing you might enjoy reading about the situations I got myself into and perhaps you may learn a thing or two, or be appalled by a thing or three.

If you decide to give it a try, remember that borders exist to be crossed, and boundaries to be vindicated. Society has convinced itself that a mere two weeks' vacation a year should do the trick, and people accept it as the norm. I don't know about you but I refuse to settle for that mindset. No matter the circumstances, I'm always good to go!

A quick disclaimer here. Let me state that I'm not a huge fan of a thing called *political correctness*. However, by no means is it my intention to offend anyone. Regardless of race, gender, ethnicity, religion or background, I treat everyone the same and all people are of equal value to me. Just so you know!

1

SWITZERLAND

An unrecognizable face, black and blue, covered in scratch marks, skin violently ripped away with blood gushing out from her head, pouring into the cracks of the sharp surrounding rocks. The limbs are twisted unnaturally, bones are bruised and broken, rotator cuff and even hip joints crushed. At an altitude of over 8,200 feet, the only thing breaking the silence is the wind, howling through the crisp cold air. Snow interspersed with a freezing drizzle; the temperature, just like the chances of survival, is dropping below zero. Will the Swiss Alps claim another victim tonight?

While dusk morphs into darkness there's little hope for this seemingly already lifeless body. While I hold the unconscious body of my best friend's sister in my arms I can feel her pulse dropping away as if the soul had surrendered, begging to let her go. Completely in shock and overwhelmed by confusion I can't get the image out of my mind: seeing a loved one falling down seventy yards, slamming into the mountain's jaws with devouring greed, even tearing up her clothes. An emergency blanket alone won't provide enough warmth, so I cover her with my jacket and soft-shell, even laying on top of her to keep the vital organs going. As I try to think of ways to carry the girl down the mountain, her body temperature is dropping below 32 degrees Celsius. In an area unknown to us despair awaits. How am I ever going to get her out of here?

A few days ago, everyone was really looking forward to this holiday abroad in the autumn. Or, should I say (in a fitting manner) in the fall? A long anticipated and well-deserved break from the already worrisome times. Family friends from the Netherlands had rented a cabin in the heights of the green hills which was on the verge of losing its luster on account of the season. Of partial Swiss descent, they were planning to visit some old relatives nearby. What a coincidence, as I had planned to climb the Jungfrau and Matterhorn, two of the many scenic snow-capped mountains the neutral gem of Switzerland has to offer. To kill two birds with one stone the idea is born to spend some time together before going our separate ways again.

I travel along serpentine railway tracks, responsible for many of my day dreams, so smooth they seemed to teleport me to romantic Zurich. Savoring the epic white landscapes from behind the window, the ride alone is worth it. After meeting up at a hotel we travel further in a spacious rental car to the idyllic village of Sigriswil which is situated between the more familiar cities of Thun and Interlaken. These cities are connected by a breathtaking marine lake, surrounded by pleasant smelling pines and typical European winding roads (always a bit too narrow). The rays of sunshine are too weak to melt the eternal snow, yet strong enough to melt our hearts. Russet cows with big bells around their necks freely roam around the quaint cabin, with suspicious aromas giving away its identity as a local cheese farm. Colorful geraniums adorn its balconies, with clear blue skies and a handful of poultry, this leisure surpasses everyone's expectations.

Little did we know that barely twenty-four hours later our joy would turn into a nightmare. That Monday morning Heidy and I decide to go for a little hike through the hills. For now we can still enjoy each other's company, soon I'm off on my solo climb which I'm very excited about (after all, my love for climbing started within these lands).

Lost in deep conversation our way becomes steeper as we go. The route appears to turn increasingly into a climb, and we obviously lack the proper equipment. Above the tree line, virgin snow collects our footprints. Patches of ice clutch smooth boulders that have been around since the beginning of times. Panting for breath, warm air from our lungs condensates into little clouds. About a hundred feet below the summit I notice my friend, whom I met during a kayaking session through the Dutch swamps, is having some difficulty with the gradient at this level of altitude. On a naturally formed nine-square-feet apron I tell her to stay put, eat something, and try to keep warm as I continue my ascension up the mountain. Once at the top, the view is magnificent with all the mountains nearby; one could relish in its pureness for days. However, I make it back within an hour because we have to return to the cabin, which is still a good three and a half hours downhill.

We're scrambling for no more than five minutes when Heidy mentions her concern over the slippery rocks. In doing so, she admits to be somewhat frightened. Naively underestimating the seriousness of the situation, I do not account for the unpredictability of the rocks. But, as the saying goes: too little, too late. By the time hesitation sinks in I try to comfort her with the assurance that I would catch her if she falls. Oh, the irony... From this moment on, and for the rest of my life, I would never say anything I know I can't follow through on because the words had hardly left my lips when she slips and falls. Sheer panic screams from her eyes as she desperately tries to grab a hold on something; scratching her fingers on the solid surface, like an animal in a cage trying to escape. I quickly grab her coat thinking that will stop her, but it's too steep to handle since she's already sliding down. In fact, I just manage to grab hold of a rock with one hand, before I could fall, too. Within seconds she tumbles down in free fall speed, and all I can do is watch. With an outstretched arm, I hang there helpless, utterly paralyzed by the sight of my friend disappearing into the nothingness. I feel the blood drain my face as I collect all my breath and scream from the top of my lungs a long and terrifying "No!" Echoes of my scream are heard throughout the entire valley. Piercing through the freezing harshness - the resonating sound of my voice fills it completely, yet even more so in my head, again and again, and a million times more; for the next hours to come, and days, weeks, and months. I'm instantly traumatized. At the same time, my body is pumping with adrenaline due to shock, so I start climbing down like a maniac putting myself at great risk.

I reach the so-called crash site as fast as I can, only to be shocked once more as she lays there – motionless. Unrecognizable as my friend or even as a human being. Due to the velocity of her fall, I'm surprised that she hadn't descended much further, because it's quite steep, however, the invisible hand of God compassionately stopped her fall. I quickly construct a small platform from nearby pebbles, preventing her from sliding further down, thus also reducing more damage to the body that is already in an unnatural position. With a bottle of water I rinse her blond locks to establish the seriousness of the wounds to her head. Someone up there must have reckoned that it was not her time yet because, after a while, she actually came to her senses, albeit in and out, due to the incredible pain and blood loss. She manages to whisper that she has a cellphone in her backpack that miraculously lies a few yards away. Although it has minimum coverage it is enough to reach the rescue center where we immediately order a helicopter. Heidy even finds enough strength to talk to the medical staff on the phone, and knowing that aid is on the way energizes her hope and revitalizes her will to survive. Unfortunately, weather conditions worsen by the minute, intensifying the situation with stronger winds and more snow.

To make things worse, the team from the rescue operation can't find us. Frustration mounts when I hear the helicopter approach and disappear again. Paired with shouting into the sky I desperately shine our Petzl head torches with both hands, but my desperate signals are not picked up. It takes a scandalous three hours before we get located. In the meantime, the whole village has come out from their houses at the foot of the mountain, watching the helicopter's searchlight canvassing the precipitous cliffs. Among the crowd, Heidy's own mother. She is holding her breath, expecting the worst as we hadn't returned yet.

I try to speak comforting and encouraging words whilst cautiously caressing the hair of my dying friend. She is slipping into unconsciousness more frequently now; her losing battle for life becomes ever more obvious. Putting down on paper what really went through my mind is a hopeless task as I was in a constant state of disbelief. We found out later that the pilot was blinded by his searchlight reflecting off the snow, which explains the hard time the pilot had in keeping his iron bird steady, even more so in those treacherous winds. One thing is for certain, the circling of the rotating blades right above us made an unforgettable and horrid noise.

But then, out of the overwhelming, unrealistic supernova overhead, a rescue worker is lowered by a cable. As soon as the soles of his boots make contact he shoots up my friend with morphine. After receiving instructions in Swiss German, we place her in a sort of a net, making sure she lies in a stable position before she is raised up, vanishing in the black of night with the I.V. still in her arm, until I can no longer hear the tedious sound of the blades.

About fifteen minutes pass until they return to pick me up, but this time connecting the cable to my harness until I go airborne. Feeling myself being reeled in I expect to be pulled into the helicopter but, squinting my eyes to look up, I see that isn't their intent. Now I'm hanging about one meter below the bottom of the helicopter on a cable that looks way too thin for my comfort. It's here I discover they don't have a hatch or anything. So there I go, still in shock, dressed in a blood-covered T-shirt amidst a freezing snowstorm while hanging in midair at over 8,200 feet. Pretty soon we arrive at a part that is just flat enough to land on. Being lowered to the ground I am immediately exchanged for Heidy who is flown off to Bern, the capital of Switzerland, four hours after the accident (the whole thing takes ridiculously long, seriously diminishing any chances of survival). Proficient surgeons however, are already on standby when she is brought in, saving crucial minutes during the several operations they perform on her that very night. Titanium plates have to hold the torn bones together. They are baffled by the fact that they can't detect any internal bleeding which is very peculiar considering the seemingly Grim Reaper provoking accident. Nevertheless she is definitely in a bad condition and to try to mitigate any further risks it is mandatory for my friend to remain in intensive care.

The moment I stagger back to the cabin Heidy's mother is still waiting outside. Finding me with her daughter's blood all over me is a gruesome sight – one can only imagine the impact of something like that. It took months of recovery in several hospitals, and months more of rehabilitation therapy which included learning how to walk again – just like that a year of your life is consumed by literally getting back on your feet.

Without a doubt, this was the most intense experience of my life. Plagued by guilt, this was a haunting experience for me as well. While I was not responsible for any of it, I definitely felt like I was. *If I had only done this or that*, are recurring regrets. Even the sound of a centrifuging washing machine, crazily resembling the unforgettable noise of rotating helicopter blades, brings me instantly back to the mountain, where I witnessed my good friend dying in agony. Having seen her fall there is little doubt there is more between heaven and earth. Because there is no way anyone could have survived that, yet she did.

Treacherous mountains almost claimed my own life on more than one occasion. This particular time, spending the night on one of the Alps around Lake Geneva, I saw something that I'll never forget. As youngsters, my buddy Chris and I were going for a summit attempt, when overnight we were barraged by a brutal hailstorm with hail the size of marbles.

Huddled up together beneath an army poncho, we place our backpacks on the outside as our last line of defense. We are scared to death when the mountain itself began to tremble with an ear-deafening clamor.

At the apex of the storm, amidst lethal circumferential winds, I can't contain my curiosity any longer and decide to check the perimeter. Clinging to a solid part of the mountain, for it's very steep where we sheltered ourselves, I flick on my flashlight. The alarming sight make my muscles tense completely, causing me to freeze. My breathing stops and a sound escapes when I frantically tried to yell. What I see can only be described as half the mountain collapsing. At a distance of twenty-five yards a huge landslide is rushing down the slope, dragging utterly anything along in its path. It is a black demon wall, meters high, consisting of massive boulders, entire trees, mud and dirt. The sheer power and magnitude of this monster are some of the most frightening things I've ever seen. I consider it pure luck that we lived to tell the tale.

And imagine this, the previous day we actually called our parents on the phone from a booth, naive as we were, announcing that if they didn't hear anything from us in the next three days, it's because we were dead. Being young and vibrant you seldom realize the concern you can cause for others.

Crazy as it may sound, this near-death experience was possibly less shocking than another experience I had with that very same friend of mine. Upon walking into his room, a little earlier than he expected, I saw him completely naked apart from his white socks. He happened to be making passionate love to his folded pillow on his bed – doggy-style. Understandably, without sharing a single word of confrontation, we never spoke of it again.

Because accidents happen you should always stay vigilant in the mountains. During one of my solo climbs to the summit of the Mont Blanc on the French side, the other half being in Italy, there is a certain area you need to cross once you pass the glacier. It's known by locals as the Death Gully because it's unstable and unpredictable to traverse.

During my successful attempt in 2014, I find myself standing in the exact middle of the gully when I notice a high-pitched sound coming from above. My ever-probing eyes spot a group of other climbers and I realize they're professionally blowing their whistles in order to warn against the oncoming danger. Yet by now it is already too late – rocks are flying inches away from where I stand. Due to the steepness and because I'm not attached to a rope I can't move quickly, neither back nor forth. But the realization kicks in that if I want to survive I have to take action, now! I take a huge risk jumping back as fast as I possibly can to hide behind the first piece of rock that sticks out a bit. Those who have been here before will know that it's a miracle that I didn't fall. Squatting down I grab my ankles to make myself as small as possible. How can I describe the overwhelming fear you experience when boulders the size of half a car come crushing by? There, right in front of you, where you were standing milliseconds ago. The dull thuds are unlike anything you will ever hear, for they are truly the sound of death. And death is a familiar past time in the rather accessible white mountain of Mont Blanc. The last time I visited Saint-Gervais-les-Bains, no less than twelve unfortunate mountaineers plummeted to their deaths that season.

During another incident, contrary to the slopes of ice, I happened to be in an invigorating climate with 83 degrees Fahrenheit, hanging on a 90-degree angled cliff on the rocky coast of the Spanish island of Ibiza, in 2002. For some reason, it seemed like a good idea at the time to free climb this baby without ropes, gear, or any form of protection at all, let alone informing anyone about the attempt. Sticking to the 60-

feet high wall at four feet below the summit I inadvertently put myself in a tight situation. Unexpectedly, the top layer of the ridge of this abyss had transformed into mere soil, as opposed to the solid dependable rocks prior.

Every pebble I try comes crumbling off. Returning was not an option, so I'm left with two choices and the outcome will literally rule over life and death. My first option is to let myself drop to be smashed onto the rocks down below in the breakers, therefore not counting as an actual option, and my second and only real option is to jump to the only piece of rock that is sticking out above me, which is a foot higher than my already stretched arm can reach, not to mention the risk of it pulling out from the loose soil by my weight – pretty much ending up at the first choice after all.

There is no shame in admitting this is one of the most fearful decisions I ever had to make. In a way, you have to find peace within yourself that there's a very good chance you're not going to make it, basically accepting that this is the moment you will die. Eventually facing reality, I go for the jump. By the grace of God, the piece of rock withstands the downforce of my weight and grants me passage to crawl over the ridge to reach the top. Laying on my sweaty back in the grass, my heart pounding in my chest, I promise myself to never undertake something so stupid again.

This event being just the tip of the iceberg of a long list of near-death experiences in the mountains, I can't really say that I learned from it or that I kept that promise. Every climber and mountaineer knows, once standing on the summit having overcome hardships and personal challenges, that the view is the greatest prize, and you know what you've been doing it for. If I have to explain this to you, you'll probably never understand the sensation. We *have* to do it.

Resuming the account of my friend Heidy for a brief moment, exactly a decade after the virulent incident; nearly completely rehabilitated from the accident in the Alps and finally having overcome the fear of mountains, she decided to take a trip to the Nepalese Himalaya. What can be more exhilarating than trekking one of the beautiful Annapurna trails in alluring Asia? Well, perhaps you'll remember this from the news, but she ended up fighting for her life once more, as her group became entangled in Nepal's worst snowstorm ever recorded, killing at least 43 people. Battling the rough forces of nature, she made it out alive – but it was a close call, enough of a story to share with journalists on a Dutch television broadcast. What I'd like to point out here is that opting for relentless travel can turn you into a true conqueror.

A stretch later, sitting among the crowd at her wedding ceremony, a shy year away from getting pregnant, and eventually becoming a mother and giving life to someone else, my eyes can't keep dry. I am incredibly thankful it didn't end there in that dark forsaken place, in the bitter cold, where she fell. Now having the opportunity to start a new generation, there is so much more in store for this amazing woman. This life is a journey of its own.

2

RUSSIA

Dark leaves are carried on winds colder than they should be this time of year. A sea of umbrellas twirl across the sodden squares as people with upturned collars go about their business in haste. Not surprisingly, no one is out longer than strictly necessary. That autumn, there seemed to be no end to the rain in the Netherlands. I'm at the shopping mall buying a planner to do some organizing. Withdrawing the blue bookmark, I open the pages to a random date: Monday, 13 March. It was as if someone from above had whispered into my ear that this was a good day to leave home, and that's exactly what happened.

Two weeks beforehand I had quit my job and started to arrange the last things for my trip: canceling insurances, getting a credit card, etcetera. At the city hall the lady behind the reception desk writes 'Emigration to China', leaving the corners of my mouth stretching from ear to ear. When you burn your bridges, you'd better do it in style, especially when embarking on a journey with the intention of finding a place to rest your weary soul. I plan nothing, except for visiting Lhasa at one point.

A friend's mother sent me a postcard with the text: "Wherever you may run to, you will always carry your past with you." Really? Inevitably the card ended up in the trash can. Does nobody understand me? Do you really want me to live my life like everyone else? Pursuing a superficial career, marrying your second choice and dealing with an insane mortgage that you have to work your ass off for?

The decision had been made and no one is able to change my mind or convince me to stay. Although I have to admit that waving farewell to family and friends as I walk through the last gates at the airport is far from easy and when out of sight I almost choke up. When I receive a text message from friends later on, it turns out that I wasn't the only one feeling sentimental. Thankfully, the excitement of boarding the airplane comforts me.

I have a two-hour layover at the airport in Vienna before I can travel on to Russia. The long check-in queue is boring, but not for long. A black briefcase is left unattended in the middle of the dome-shaped hall and apparently, I'm not the only one to notice it. Security guards flock from all directions. A loud buzzer is the green light for the sloppy evacuation that follows. Everyone remains calm and actually acts quite sober. Hallelujah that organized terrorism wasn't such a big topic back then.

Waking up in the capital city of the former Soviet Union is surreal as the sheer amount of snow is remarkable. Even the cars are fully covered, sporadically only a roof shows itself as the thick white blanket has Moscow in a half nelson.

The previous day people at the airport were waiting for certain tourists holding up a sign with their name. I'm sure you've seen them. Wouldn't it be nice if you pretended to be someone else just to see where you'll end up? Sometimes I have to restrain myself from doing anything stupid. Anyway, I am carrying way too much luggage with me – what was I thinking? Falling for the same trap any new traveler does. My backpack is unbearable, not to mention the other backpack I brought along. It's a process. Let's leave it at that.

The tiles at overcrowded metro stations still bear signs of the old Communist regime, you can't look anywhere without being confronted with red hammers and sickles. It's unimaginable how many lives had to suffer from this concealed part of history. Perhaps this is why people's faces look so miserable.

Without a map I swirl through the, mostly grim, city. Noticing that all buildings are alike, I think they must have hijacked the blueprints of one architect and kept on reusing it for all the buildings in the entire area. Walking on cobblestones in the city center I stumble upon the world-famous Red Square, for years the stage of national ceremonies and thriller screenplays. Decorations and symbols are all over the Kremlin Palace; the huge red walls symbolizing the power of the bear. Even if you know nothing about the country, everybody would recognize those colorful vortex-shaped towers of the St. Basil Cathedral. Filming inside is illegal, however upon entering, it is needless to say that I do it anyway.

While filming on my camera, the cathedral transports me back many years ago to when I visited the Sistine Chapel in Rome where I did the same. That time, security personnel detected what I was doing and chased me down the corridor with clubs in their hands, luckily, they never got me.

Nearby lies the embalmed corpse of Lenin, of all things. To some a hero, to many a true dictator, and to me not worth paying last respects to. After all, this sick-minded bastard committed horrendous crimes that he was never charged with, so I think I'll skip it for now as there are plenty of other things to see. A man across the square poses with a live eagle on his arm; a magnificent creature. Innumerable salesmen desperately try to flog me with fur hats from the Russian army. Surely their income isn't a fortune so, albeit annoying, I can't really blame them for pursuing me. My matching Fjällräven outfit is overly touristy.

Moscow's wintertime does not inspire one to linger about. Moreover, an important condition for a visa was to play by their rules, so I'm kind of on a schedule here. Leaving the chaos of the Third Rome, as the city is sometimes referred to, I decide to pick a train for transportation since public services are fairly well organized.

Taking the Golden Ring Route from Vladimir to Suzdal, more or less a hundred kilometers away, there is no chance of growing indifferent. Talk about a scenic route! Snowy landscapes lead to the Byzantine Orthodox place of pilgrimage, which is characterized by the number of churches, monasteries and several other intriguing palaces with gentle, soft colors; the best maintained ones in all of Russia. Being far away from urban areas the notable quietness assures a good night's sleep.

The morning light makes me open up the hatches of my log cabin to this open-air museum. Woodcarvings on the facades are a treat to the eye for this carpenter. At night, an open fire heats my ready-to-use meal that I brought from home. I receive strange looks from the proprietor of the estate as he passes, he is probably wondering why I'm not dining in the restaurant like the other guests. Not that I understand anything on the menu, the thirty-six characters of the Russian alphabet are as incomprehensible to me as braille. I'm still astonished by the amount of snow; I never expected a quantity of this size could come down in one season. Now, with spring at the threshold, the weather is predominantly sunny. On my last day in the region I visit a Kremlin from the eleventh century with captivating building techniques, an ode to the remnants of Gog and Magog.

With the life I left behind fresh in mind I board the train that will take me thousands of miles eastward. And not just any train but the highly popular Trans-Siberian Express! Shoving down my luggage beneath one of the beds it becomes obvious that this compartment is very small: there are four beds in total with two on either side. Unfortunately, I am too tall to stretch out my body, which means I have to sleep curled up. To make matters worse, the old railroad car makes a lot of noise during the night. At the break of dawn everything starts to look better except me because I didn't get a wink of sleep. A tiny mirror in my compass reflects my sleep deprived face. Yet, the view of ever-changing landscapes is breathtaking. A little north of Kazakhstan the route goes right through the Ural.

Endless plains and dense forests are never boring. The same goes for mountains clothed in sheets of pine trees and solid frozen lakes. Every five hundred kilometers or so styles of houses differ totally. In one area, all of them are made from rocks, in another area solely from hewn logs. I guess they use whatever is available in that particular district. We only make a few stops a day, sometimes for five minutes, sometimes twenty, but never for very longer. At those moments, it's a delight to catch a breath of fresh air. On the side of the sorrowful platforms old ladies try to sell home-cooked dishes for a pittance. Judging from their tattered clothing it's a struggle to get by. Most of the time I have no idea what I'm eating but it's not too bad actually. A portion of dried fish however is delicious.

In the bed opposite my compartment sits a dude from Mongolia. No offense, but gosh that poor guy is ugly: his head is huge and looks like a pumpkin – that would be the perfect nickname for his girlfriend to call him. Anyway, in the bed above him lies a young Russian. How do I get across to him that I don't appreciate him making loud phone calls at night? Neither of them speak a word of English. For days on end we stare at each other until communication finally starts, thanks to my initiative I might add. As the journey progresses we actually get to know everything about each other. Where we reside, our professions, if we have siblings or even children, if we're married – everything. Amazing how much you learn from talking with your hands and feet. It can take some effort but the upside is that you tap into creativity you didn't even know you possessed. Now that the ice is broken we even share our food and provisions. Using improvised instruments we make music and sing songs we all know. I have barely left home and already I'm entangled in experiences that become memories for life – one of the great perks of backpacking.

After passing a few time zones, we show up at the notable city of

Irkutsk. Dizzy from the long ride the freezing temperatures outside do me good. Once more my outfit is to blame for instantly being identified as a tourist. Cab drivers attack like a pack of wild hyenas but as long as someone carries my overweight luggage I don't really care where I step into. Not that my demands are very high; all the available cars seem to be falling apart. Two guys with stereotypical square heads take me to Listvianka. One of them has a fun fact about the paved road we drive on. In poor English and a thick accent he explains that it is the only paved road in the area. A few years back a foreign presidential visit was planned, but cancelled at the very last moment. However, the road that acted as a propaganda stunt was already laid! How about that?

When the taxicab drops me off in front of an affordable log cabin I think, *smell you later!* Entering the cabin, I throw my luggage in the corner and walk double-quick towards my dream that appears out of the rising mist across the street. Truly awe inspiring, the magical Lake Baykal, which according to legend, is the oldest and deepest lake in the world. Nature in its purest form, the fresh scents of evergreens fill my lungs. What a scene! I decide to go out immediately. Everyone takes advantage of the ice that is meters thick, very solid and flat as a pancake. Semi-trucks have found their shortcut, not having to drive around the lake, and motorcycles and SUVs are having fun on the slippery surface, even the army transport soldiers in their snazzy new toy, a genuine hovercraft. I've got to get me one of those! Supercool. As if that isn't enough a dog sled with a pack of huskies comes along. I just watch them for now since paying for a ride is rather expensive. Further ahead a group of men with fur hats encircle a hole they've cut in the ice. Holding fishing rods with anticipation, the big handsaw still lying next to them. The fish they catch go by the name of *omul*. Apparently, this species only lives in Lake Baykal. According to a century-old tradition it is smoked on the shore at local markets that emerged when the settlers realized the importance of the lake. The fish smells like it tastes; delicious. I don't know what else to compare it to.

A woman starts talking to me in German, but I assure her that I am from a place where they don't speak that language. It must be my blond hair and blue eyes that led her to that assumption. On the way back to my cabin I hike up a steep hill to fully enjoy the swift sunset. With nightfall approaching a miracle unfolds as I have never seen nor would ever see again afterwards. In the little time I spent there, the heavens were completely transformed, as if I was watching through a gigantic lens, reaching beyond galaxies. The quantity of stars is indescribable; not a piece of black sky remains, it's all one bright twinkling festival.

Back on the Trans-Siberian Express everything is small. Small compartment, small bathroom, small hallway, except for the conductress who is huge and hardly fits through the narrow doorways. I have sympathy for her shoes as her ankles resemble tree trunks. Speaking about shoes, it is interesting that every woman in this country seems to be wearing heels. Even the children start off having about one inch of heel, the younger women of course wear high heels, and the old ladies wear variable sizes, yet never a flat sole. I really like these overly feminine features incorporated in their culture. In the countryside you will never see a woman wearing pants, but rather a dress or skirt. Just like pretty much all other Russians on the train the mouth of the conductress is filled with golden teeth. And I can only imagine as to why; they swallow entire bottles of vodka as early as seven in the morning. They drink it like it's water.

Through scratched windows I thoughtlessly gaze into the distance. Tumble weeds are rolling along and every now and then a whirlwind sweeps the surroundings. I am baffled by the number of oil refineries – huge pumps bedeck fields for days on end. Just imagine how much oil that generates. This time I'm sharing my compartment with three

Chinese dudes. My, my, my, they were downright disgusting. They clip their nails anywhere they please, spit on the floor and gargle through their nose as if they are trying to loogie their lungs out. They smack their lips while eating, not to mention the kind of things they eat! Raw chicken feet complete with the yellow skin is still tolerant, but why would anyone on earth eat pig snout? They come in packs of three, saturated in gelatin, one hundred percent grease. Rumor has it you are what you eat; their shiny faces prove the statement to be true. Spat-out sunflower seed shells litter the entire floor and by now I don't even wish to know what their homes look like. Have you ever seen someone taking a handful of sunflower seeds and sort out the shell and seed in their mouth? I don't know how they do it. Incongruous with their disgusting habits, they are exceptionally kind. These funny lads with a graceful yet clear slant in their eyes also propose to share their food but I politely decline.

Suddenly one of them beckons me to follow him. Curious about what he has to offer I tail him several wagons down the hallway. It all becomes clear when he introduces me to the only other westerner on the whole freaking train. It is such a relief to speak English again that our conversation lasts five unremitted hours. The young British man and I enjoy the comfort of verbal communication; we almost forgot how much we took a fast and easy conversation for granted. The next day we force the lock of a door in a narrow, abandoned foyer. To our surprise we find a closet full of old conductor uniforms, complete with communist emblems! We dress up in the blue trench coats and salute one another in made-up Russian words. We even snap a few pictures.

On passing platforms a lot of trading takes place. Salesmen are very competent at selling their goods as speed is a primary requirement since the train only stops for a few minutes. Merchandise consists of blankets and pillows, clothing in all shapes and colors, and even plastic kids toys and cosmetic products. Sticking my head out of the top part of a window I follow it all from up close. Not only do they work on these overcrowded platforms between so much junk, some actually live there in poorly constructed tents. I wouldn't want to stand in their shoes, it is hard to imagine this tough and stressful way of living never seems to cease.

By now the faces of the people have drastically changed. The Euro-look is nowhere to be found anymore; we are the only Caucasians and everyone else is straight-up Asian.

Returning to my own compartment at night the Chinese are already sleeping. It doesn't take long for me to doze off myself. In the middle of the night I wake up scared half to death. The windows are steamed up when I slide the pale green curtains aside to see where this eerie noise is coming from. Gruff soldiers march through the aisles with German shepherds sniffing anything their noses come across. That sure wakes me up.

A loud Russian voice – at the time gibberish to me – rattles through a shrill speaker, obnoxiously hurting my ears. What the hell is happening? I anxiously try to figure it out; it feels as if we had gone back in time by a couple of decades. When the soldiers start yelling I begin to get really nervous. Wiping the sleep from my eyes I try to look as innocent as possible. All passports are thrown into a cardboard box as soldiers force everyone off the train, without any belongings. In a split second I grab my jacket and toque which turns out to be a very wise decision. Temperatures have dropped to minus 25 degrees Celsius! Station lights cut through the darkness, they blind my eyes and reveal the clouds of breath coming out of our mouths. Then it becomes clear that we are at the border to China.

Slick figures surround me to intrusively request changing money. They want my rubles in exchange for *renminbi*, which is yuan although they call it *kuai*. One individual, his black greasy hair combed to the back, has a seemingly low exchange rate. But I guess at these moments it's always a complete rip-off. Better to choose one and forget about it.

A group of Chinese teenagers invite me to join them in search of something edible. After a moment of hesitation, I agree to come along.

For hours on end we walk through no man's land in the black of night. Not knowing where I am, not having my passport on me and unable to speak the language, felt as though I had no identity. You're damn right that's exciting!

In a musty store with items stashed to the ceiling we buy dried fish and biscuits, candy, coca cola and chewing gum. Judging from the wrappers alone the items are leftovers from the Second World War. Salesmen look at me as if they're seeing a honky for the first time in real life. And who knows? We divide the food until it's equally distributed. This strikes a sensitive cord with me; the group mentality is a world of difference compared to the egocentric West, where everyone is individualistic and me-centered.

For a moment, I'm taken back to a memory of eastern Europe's Romania where I volunteered several times and worked with drug addicts, street children, and at orphanages. When I gave a sandwich to one of the homeless kids he immediately shared the bread with his friends instead of stuffing it directly into his own mouth. Things like that are hard to forget. It made me think twice about certain things.

Having returned to the train station we have to wait forever. China is the only country in the world with different rail tracks. Unbelievably, there are huge cranes that lift up the disengaged wagons a meter above the ground so that underpaid workers labor hard to change the wheels. This is definitely something crazy to witness.

At this point, I seriously begin to wonder if I will ever be reunited with my belongings. Luckily, we are summoned to return to the railroad cars. Climbing on board it is always a pleasure to find your backpack scrutinized and badly repacked by the authorities. After half a day of waiting I am proud as a monkey with seven dicks to have my passport back with new stamps of the Orient. I officially crossed the border!

3

CHINA

Panoramas of white meadows and snowy hills are captivating. Literally nothing looks like back home anymore. At the front, at the back, next to the wagon at the adjacent tracks and beneath, there is no escaping the tons of steel shooting by, accompanied by millions of wooden beams. If you even try to compare this train ride to those through the Swiss Alps, you are mistaken. There is little to no comparison to the Trans-Siberian Express, because it's so noisy and unrelenting. However, bonding with the group of Chinese teenagers I previously met at the border has been heartwarming and for that reason I am sad to see them leave when they step off at Harbin, the city famous for the world's biggest annual exhibition of ice sculptures.

While traveling around the outer borders of Mongolia I realize that we are so far to the east it almost becomes west again on the other side of the world, close to Alaska. Therefore, it took a while for us to finally hit the dazzling capital.

Then, early in the morning, at twenty past five to be precise, fresh air welcomes me to Beijing, previously known as Peking. The Chinese hostess that comes to pick up the young British man that I met on the train, warns me to carefully watch my money. She goes on to explain that thieves will easily recognize me as a tourist due to my big nose. *Gee, any other compliments you want to make?* I think to myself while frowning. I am sure my massive backpack, blond hair and blue eyes will go completely unnoticed!

As we go our separate ways, it suddenly hits me that I'm entirely by myself in a foreign country far away from anything familiar. Standing in the middle of the street, I can no longer rely on the safety of the train, yet it is comforting to know what can happen when you are aimlessly going about, for it doesn't take long for me to stumble upon a random hostel, where I immediately check-in.

Getting some cash at a nearby back, the receipt from the ATM announces my new life as a millionaire in China: one US dollar equals ten yuan, ten US dollars equals a hundred, and a hundred US dollars equals a thousand yuan. Long live capitalism! Completely exhausted by sitting in a crappy train for weeks I sink into my bed, an actual bed, even one that I can finally stretch out in and catch up the lost hours of sleep.

It is unsure whether or not there really are nine million bicycles in Beijing, but at this moment in history, there really are over seventeen million inhabitants living in the capital city of China. You would think that with so many people, the city would be in disarray, and it is. However, the main streets do not display much disorder as they are neat and tidy. All day long, women with facemasks against the pollution, clean up the streets with brooms made of twigs. Most tourists' gazes focus solely on the well-maintained parks and buildings. No poverty to be detected. On smogless days it looks very clean and modern. Yet, behind all the glory of misleading facades, real life begins to seep through the exterior in the back streets and narrow alleys. Mud and food waste fill dirt roads and houses seem about to collapse. Underfed locals in worn-out clothing watch me from the corner of their eyes. Out of shame I feel incapable of snapping some shots. Hungry stares of children haunt me; the look in their eyes presumably as hollow as their stomachs. In the suburbs everyone looks strung-out; conditions are worse than ever and not all of them will reach a good old age.

While intentionally getting lost I roam about the city. Traffic signs are unreadable. Even with the Chinese language course I took, most people have no idea what I am trying to say. The intonation of syllables is of extreme importance in Mandarin and unfortunately, I do not reach a lot further beyond "Ni hao!" Lost in thought I chance upon Tiananmen Square. Some of you will probably recall images of the demonstration that ended violently in 1989. Several students ask politely if they can practice their English, and although it's not my first language I like to believe I speak it fluently. Others boldly request a picture, which is as flattering as it is amusing.

With twenty degrees Celsius it's almost a fifty-degree difference in temperature from a few days ago, so I was sweating my ass off. Opposite the square stand the imposing walls of the Forbidden City. Parallel with the walls pink-blossomed trees give off an incredible sweet smell, providing a gentle contrast to the many brusque and dignified looking dragon statues. Above the arch-shaped entrance is a huge painting of the Communist dictator Mao Zedong. If leaders from the old dynasties had known that it would have come to this, they would have burned their empires down to the ground. No less than fifty million deaths to his name and here he is worshipped like a god. Some revolution, eh?

In spite of it all, it is great to snoop around. Deep red walls are provocative, as are the mighty, curved roofs of palatial architecture, symbolizing their power and early advancements. Since childhood I have always dreamt of visiting this palace, which is a UNESCO World Heritage site for obvious reasons. It is truly a privilege to stand in the inner courts of a place with such a rich history.

My following experience will forever be linked to the Forbidden

City because it all started within its walls. Two students from Xian invite me over for a cup of tea, a common habit in Chinese culture. Having a weakness for Asian girls I agree to join. They are in town to visit some friends and when I inquire where those friends are they quickly answer: "At home!" Fair enough. Through a jumble of streets we keep on walking until we enter a pharmacy. At the end of the store, a spiraling stairway takes us to the next floor where the magic begins. Wallpaper and candles make for a flashy entrance. A charming lady in a tight cheongsam lures us into a small, secret chamber. The three of them are all very talkative but I have no idea what they are saying. Seemingly in admiration, they shower me with compliments. Within the luxurious chamber the charming lady pours at least thirty tiny cups of tea, all with a different herb. This goes on for an hour and a half, and I am having the time of my life. Upon leaving, the girls suggest I treat them for this day and ask me to take care of the bill. *How expensive can it be?* Without any suspicion, I pay the bill and once outside we go our separate ways.

Walking back to my hostel I come across a bank, which has a sign on the sidewalk with the exchange rates. As I had just arrived, I had not fully done the math yet. Then it suddenly hits me. In my mind I return to the tea place and see the credit card sticker on the door. Recalling the private chamber and awkward praises I received, I realize that I had been scammed. I gave those girls an entire month of wages!

Back at the hostel, I feel like an idiot and end up having a restless night. Clothed in shame I tell my unfortunate event to an Irish tourist in my dormitory – I just had to get it off my chest. I cannot believe my ears when he tells me that two days ago they swindled him, too! *Okay, this means war.* With tingling veins and my blood boiling, I forge a strategy to catch those little rats. *It is payback time.*

Early the next day I position myself on the side of Tiananmen Square, disguised in a different outfit, hiding in the crowd and slightly earlier from when we met the previous day. I am thoroughly convinced they collaborate with the teahouse, gathering and scamming new victims every day. Now the goal is to catch them red handed, confront them and demand my hard-earned cash back.

As predicted, the fake students from Xian show up. The feeling that surfaces upon seeing the thieves is indefinable. Feeling like Jason Bourne himself I shadow them for twenty minutes traversing the square all the way into the Forbidden City. Keeping a distance of about thirty feet I have to be patient until they strike.

Scouting the area for a new victim one of them looks straight into my blood-red eyes, grabs her friend and they start running as fast as they can. However, those little paws are no match for my Dutch legs and it doesn't take long for me to catch up and grab them by the necks, a firm grip with my relatively big hands. When I ask for an explanation on why they are trying to avoid me, they start screaming their lungs out. Great, now a large group of bystanders encircle us, which includes some authority figures. Oddly enough, they keep their distance and just stand there watching. The tallest Chinese around starts threatening me but I am still a head taller so I ignore him completely. After bystanders listen to my explanation everyone is on their way again, as if nothing had ever happened. Those Chinese... I tell you.

Then we walk back through the Beijing labyrinths and into the teahouse. Kicking in the door certainly stirs a commotion. When I confront the manager he is not easily persuaded, undoubtedly protecting his employees and not giving in to unmasking his clandestine operations. Threatening to call the police helps, and the adventure ends with getting a refund, or better put, I gain what was rightfully mine to begin with. In spite of all the evidence, they keep denying my accusations. They are probably scamming unsuspecting tourists to this very day.

Well-known and lesser-known buildings are all trapped in scaffolding. Renovation works are in full force. We are still more than two years away from the Olympic Games that will be held in 2008, but as of yet the country is overrun with billboards and all kinds of advertisements promoting the event. For now, one can still obtain illegal DVDs on the street for peanuts, and together with other tourists we watch them in the hostel. Some of the guests have already been traveling for months. I envy them, still unaware that I will greatly exceed most of them. At the reception of the hostel everyone laughs at me, for the other day I accidentally chewed on a red pepper during supper and steam came out of my ears!

Personnel from the hostel show me a good deal for a guided tour of the Great Wall but when they disclose that it's only a five-hour hike I turn it down. It would be a shame to skimp this two-thousand-year-old structure, one of the wonders of antiquity and, once again, well-deserved UNESCO material. Unintentionally I venture forth as a lone wolf. If I want something I go for it, even if no one cares to join.

An ultra-modern subway drops me off at a bus station. Well, actually it is not really a station, but more like the whole length of the street. I jump onto a bus which I think is going in the right direction. Climbing over sacks, bags and boxes there is exactly one seat left at the very back. Smelly odors roam freely. The hired help from the driver collects money from the passengers. You have to give the kid some credit, as he has to remember exactly how much change each passenger should get – that skill alone should hopefully get him a better job in the future. Along the way, one can't help notice the number of statues of Mao. Why do they keep the memory of that miserable beast so alive? Mass indoctrination has residents believe that he was not such a bad bloke after all.

After the bus ride, I share a van with a handful of Chinese youngsters who have a trick up their sleeve. Arriving at our destination the boys turn out to be penniless and now the driver demands the whole sum from me alone, but I give him my share and start walking. He begins to chase me aggressively until I turn around and take a few steps toward him with an angry look on my face. No words needed. The tiny man realizes he does not stand a chance. I have compassion for some people, so I am happy to give them a tip. Too bad for this man who almost killed me in traffic with his crazy, irresponsible driving. During that ride alone I had about 36 near-death experiences, and that's no exaggeration. Walking in the same direction the youngsters invite me to spend the night at one of their homes. Not trusting them one bit my feet keep on walking.

About an hour later, I approach the man-made structure that I have always dreamt of visiting. As dusk falls the silhouette of my reason for being here becomes visible. Passionately anxious my heart starts beating faster until I'm finally right in front of it. With closed eyes I take a deep breath and place my left boot on the first step. Pain and sorrow penetrate my heart as if everyone from my past could see me now. I remember all those people who bullied me thinking I would never make it. Remembering all those people who said I am a nobody and a failure. Too many so-called close friends who had no faith in me, including my closest relatives. Yet here I am putting them all to shame. I feel like the king of the world. In a time before it was trendy to go to Asia and way before airline companies started throwing with insane discount deals of chartered flights, I am really standing on the Great Wall of China, and there is no living soul in the area to disturb me! Only the beautiful pheasants going about their business. Ascending the stairs with a cautious smile and a tear rolling down my cheek, I feel like I am that three-year-old boy again running away from home.

After a long period of scaling the countless stairs, the sand on the stones grind beneath my soles. As night sets in rapidly, I prepare a place to sleep in one of the collapsed watchtowers. I blow out my tea light and contently fall asleep beneath a starry sky. At five in the morning, I am forced to pack and relocate due to an instant downpour. Yet nothing can break my spirit.

The first curious rays of sunshine warm my face, while the birds begin to sing until the rusty mountains gain color. Days go by as I make my way along the Great Wall. The souls of tens-of-thousands of men soar before me into the lonely night sky; the men that fell during its laborious construction, their bodies gruesomely used as mortar being bricked into the wall. From Jingshanling to Simatai and beyond, this marvelous structure flows over ridges like a huge serpent. Some parts are destroyed, while other parts are reconstructed to keep tourism flowing.

Speaking about tourism, every day I am harassed by women who stalk me, repeatedly yelling: "Teesyure, teesyure!" As days pass, I realize they are actually trying to sell me a T-shirt.

During the walk I stumble upon four green uniforms, the guards protecting the area. Fascinated by each other we sit down to share our food, including sunflower seeds! In fact, our acquaintance is so pleasant that we spend all day together, with them teaching me several card games. When evening falls, they summon me to go down with them, as it is illegal to stay at night. Thoughtful as I am, I convince them that I only desire to make pictures of the beautiful sunset, and will follow soon. In this fashion I continue my journey for a whole week before I return to Beijing.

Memories last a lifetime, like the time I had to run from a swarm of bees, or the time I had to wipe my ass with an old pair of socks because there was nothing else to use. I remember the campfires, the millions of stairs, all the times when random strangers asked if they could take a picture with me, and all the travelers I met along the way and the stories they told. I have never been away from home for as long as I have now and the best thing is that I have no intention to go back. I absolutely love it!

Massive walls were a necessity; this dynasty had to protect itself against giants and dragons that lived in those days. Something else they had for protection was a great army. Honored by their master Qin Shi Huangdi they live forever in the form of the Terracotta Army in the city of Xian. Thousands of clay action figures and not a single one bares the same resemblance to another! I never travel with a guidebook because I love to leave it up to chance; this attitude often gets you to places no one else ventures to go. The downside of this tactic is you might accidentally miss a thing or two, as I find out the hard way when I long left Xian without having seen the Terracotta Army for myself.

A two-day train ride is next on the menu. Before I hop on I make sure to bring enough batteries for my Sony Disc-man – yes, call me old fashioned but I don't care. My compartment has six beds this time, three on either side, one above the other. It is far from comfortable but it is the cheapest I could find.

Upon arrival in Chengdu, I get a slap in the face by Mother Nature. I delve from an air-conditioned train straight into tropical temperatures, and the humidity causes streams of sweat to run down my back. In spite of the city's reputation of being well travelled by foreigners, everybody is checking me out. For some reason, they cannot keep their eyes off me which is very uncomfortable. The awning of a restaurant terrace should provide shelter, or so I think.

I feast on a big plate of tasty rice and veggies when a man approaches. Despite his unsolicited arrival he takes a chair and joins my table. Out of a black shoulder bag he conjures brochures of hotels and places to stay. Repeatedly I let this individual know that I am not interested. Later on, a police officer points out the way to the bus station, finally someone who understands my Chinese. Still being stalked by the pushy man who insists on buying my ticket, I refuse. Getting out of the bus after thirty minutes, he is still following me but this time the man maintains a proper distance, probably due to angry looks I throw at him. A rickshaw drops me off at a hostel, at last. While checking in, the man appears yet again and starts talking to staff behind the reception desk. Now it becomes clear: he tells the staff that he recommended this place and guided me here – he wants to get cash! Obviously, I came here by myself. Once explained to the staff they attempt to send him on his way. However, he has no intention to go and starts getting angry to the point of provoking me. All I can say is, do not try these tricks with someone with a short temper such as myself. I rush toward him and push him so hard he rolls across the ground of the inner courtyard. Just when I am about to lash out at him again, he runs off. Tenacious as he is, five minutes later he returns at the gate and continues his preposterous act, prompting the staff of the hostel to call the police. When they arrive the rascal is long gone but the interrogation which followed paints me as if I were the guilty one here. They check my passport and gaze at my visa for so long, that it starts making me feel uncomfortable. All my information is being recorded. By the time I roll my finger through the sticky black ink for my fingerprints, I think to myself, *great, just an hour in Chendu and I am already "most wanted" by the cops!*

Spending mornings in one of the many parks is a true delight. Hordes of locals are lined up doing synchronized gymnastics, from businessmen in suits to fanatics in sweat suits. In addition, there are karaoke bars everywhere; out of tune voices know no shame. Older couples are dancing as if it were their last time and I can watch them for hours. A nearby halfway house is well known for its panda bears. Apart from frolicking and nibbling bamboo there is not a whole lot of action going on – *but boy are they cute.*

Longing to see more of the third largest country in the world I hop on a bus to head towards the mountains. Idiotic bus drivers are playing with our lives by making a game out of who will arrive first. Doing so dangerously, they navigate through mountains with narrow paths and deep ravines. Little wonder why news headlines often include tourists dying due to some horrible accident in China. Miraculously we make it out alive. Traveling for a few good hours the tropical climate has dropped to uncomfortable temperatures. The streets and streams of Songpan are quaint. Overwhelmed by the serenity of the remote village a sigh of contentment is released into the cold air. That same air carries relaxing fragrances of fireplaces, one of my personal favorite smells. Unfortunately, there is a problem with the electricity and with the boiler in my hotel, so it takes five thick blankets to stay warm at night. Other guests are clattering around with candles. Despite the troubles the true purpose of being in the village presents itself the next morning.

For the first time in my life I go horseback riding. Straight into the hazing and not just a few hours but of couple of days! I confess that it does take some time to get used to having a stallion between your legs; that is, the horse, just to be clear. For instance, it is definitely not a car with the comfort of a steering wheel. However, I learn quickly and feel quite comfortable except for when we walk alongside steep cliffs. We start out with a group of six, consisting of three guides, a young couple from Austria and me. Although Austria is obscured in snow in the wintertime, the couple bail out in the evening, stating it is too cold for them. Yeah right, and they also landed on the moon in 1969. Not that I care, it just turned into a private tour for the same price. Towering evergreens on the hillside, crystal clear springs and naturally eroded ponds of bright aquamarine are scattered across the scenery. The view is nothing less than breathtaking. Late in the afternoon we arrive at a wooden shack that would be our home for the night. Before sunset clouds roll in and turn the dry day into a fairytale with the first flakes of snow. My versatile guides are preparing a hefty meal with big chunks of vegetables, stirring an iron cauldron with a twig. The cauldron rests above a menacing fire. Any responsible person would think that's not the wisest thing to do in a wooden shack! It does make the interior cozy though.

Outside it is snowing considerably now, erasing our tracks. Before crawling into my sleeping bag I check on the horses outside. Wiping the snow off their backs I speak encouraging words, feeling sorry for them as they have to endure the cold. While doing so I unexpectedly come face to face with a herd of yaks. The longhaired cows silently march toward the pines to seek shelter beneath dense branches. With the absence of a shepherd, they could well be wild cattle.

On the last day of the three-day trip, I am still plucking icicles out of the horse's hair. With my toes turned to stone this trip has taught me to never wear sneakers in areas with unpredictable weather. I would not want to have missed this opportunity, but stepping off to bring Shadowfax back to the stables, I sure don't mind airing the family jewels again!

Flight tickets from Chengdu to Lhasa are very cheap on purpose. Authorities will try everything for tourists to skip this extended patch of land. However, I have set my mind on doing just that: going overland to the capital of Tibet! What are they hiding there that we aren't allowed to see? Chilling in a backpackers' café, I am working on my travel plans, making notes in my organizer while chewing on the back of the pen a bit. Then something happens that will change the course of my life for the coming two months.

A haggard-looking guy with dark curls and dark shabby beard, carrying even more luggage than I have, stumbles into the café. There's a foot of snow outside and this guy is wearing flip-flops, his jeans wet up to the knees. Out of all the tables around he joins mine as if it is preordained. That very morning he was kicked out of a park by the police, almost getting himself arrested for illegally pitching his tent. Shivering from mild hypothermia he inquires about my plans. I indulge his curiosity by laying out my plan for making long-held dreams come true: I intended to buy a motorcycle to drive to the capital of a people with an abundantly rich and ancient legacy; through the forbidden lands of mystical Tibet.

His reaction unleashes an adventure which I can only hope they make into a film one day. He yells: "Dude that's wicked. I'm with you!", spattering his saliva around while his eyes almost double in size. Oddly enough, this stranger and I have been sharing pretty much the same dream. The chance to realize this impossible goal is now closer than ever. This is how I met Steve from Canada.

We travel back to Chengdu on Good Friday in the rain. I return to the hostel I was staying at before, where half of my luggage is stored. At night in the inner court I run into a familiar face. It is a man that I met before in Beijing where we had a brief conversation. We chat away about interim travels when all of a sudden he tells me he had this crazy experience. As he skittishly looks around he confesses, "When I was visiting the Forbidden City I was invited to go for a cup of tea by two students from Xian…"

On Easter Monday Steve and I find ourselves on the backseat of a police car. In order to understand why we ended up there, we need to backtrack a little. You see, my international driver's license is valid in almost the whole world, except for China. Therefore, obtaining a counterfeit license became a genuine option. I mean, they copy everything you can imagine. What manufactured product nowadays does not read *Made in China*, right? After reconsidering, we decided to gain a legitimate license, but how in the world does one acquire a Chinese license as fast as possible? Needless to say, I was not planning in taking any lessons, if they even let me have them in the first place, being a foreigner. On a quest for some clarification on what to do, a taxi brings us to a police station where we find dumb faces instead of answers. They seem to be more interested in the bucket of ice-cream they are sharing instead of helping us out. Going from station to station, we understand there are a few strings attached. Still, we are willing to follow instructions, thus ending up in the police car. Officers are kind enough to give us a ride to the traffic center. Upon arrival we were appalled by billboards of graphic traffic accidents. Is seeing ripped-apart bodies underneath blood-smeared truck tires really beneficial to anyone?

Don't ask me how but we convince the workers at the traffic center that our current licenses include driving motorcycles, which it does not. Well played! It saves us a practical test! Nevertheless, we still need to do a theoretical test and many days of frustration follow. While passport photos and copies of ID are easily dealt with, our papers must be filled out by the police, which is a real pain in the ass. So again, we go from station to station until we finally reach the right one. All the while hardly anyone speaks English. Luckily, we receive help from the owner of the Dragon Town hostel and The Loft. This man definitely deserves credit for his patience and kindness – a trait I found uncommon in many Chinese (not generalizing a billion people). We are thankful but not done yet as a physical examination still awaits at the hospital. Arriving at five past noon we learn that the doors are closed for the next couple of hours. The only thing you can do in such a situation is wait, and once more, our patience is put to the test. By the time nurses are ready to receive us about thirty men push their way in and cut the line, or rather the absence of it. Everyone elbows his or her way through. Just when we think this is not going to work we run into a resident who speaks perfect English. For reasons unknown, he offers to help, and that is exactly what he does. We go from room to room because the doctors refuse to help us until a man in a casual outfit gives us all the right papers, for a modest donation. Long live the bureaucracy! Now we have everything to start our test.

Our enthusiasm drains as time goes by, day upon day we fail our test. It is obvious that the regime is playing tricks on us and I am sure they intentionally let us fail. Options to get our license legally diminish, so desperate times call for desperate measures.

My new Canadian friend got hold of a business card from a certain Mister Lee – apparently the guy who can get things done. We make some calls and discuss if we should meet up, which we do the next day somewhere downtown, or as some poorly translated signs read, *towndown*. We dress nicely for the occasion. Mister Lee looks a bit nerdy and wears a shoulder bag with a printed hammer and sickle. Just coming from Russia myself, I ask if he bought the bag over there but he replies "No I didn't", and without turning his head he continues his motivation with: "It is communism on the outside yet all capitalism on the inside!" Steve looks at me with fear in his eyes. Now we know we are dealing with a serious motherfucker, so to speak. What have we gotten ourselves into?

Because we are not entirely sure about the situation we decide that it would be better to be up-front about everything, so we tell him our plans. Awaiting our drinks in a fancy restaurant he arranges a meeting with someone whom he thinks can help us, a certain Mister Tang. Clueless of what to expect our nerves become tenser until the moment he arrives. An ever increasing rumbling of engines draw near.

We cannot believe our eyes when three individuals drive their dirt bikes straight into the restaurant! Parking in between tables and chairs, anxious employees haste to provide food and drinks. This has to be a notorious Mob gang. As we begin to introduce ourselves to one another we try to stay as calm as possible. True colors are hard to hide, and we are sweating profusely out of places we didn't even know we could sweat from. English not being the strongest skill of our newcomer, we have our representative as interpreter. Long story short, they advise us to return to the traffic center and go by the book. The authorities already know us, so if they catch us with counterfeit material we face certain jail time and that's a risk we're not willing to take. However, things get interesting when they assure us that tomorrow we will have our licenses. Who are these people?

Reappearing at the traffic center, a man riding a rickshaw laughs in our faces, he sees us every day so he knows we are repeatedly failing the test. Entering the huge examination room there are about three hundred participants. It's basically endless rows of tables in a hangar-like building. As usual we sit all the way at the front on the right-hand side, close to the entrance, but this time two other white guys are placed next to us. They let us know they failed even more times than we did so far; it seems that the regime is not particularly fond of westerners, or am I saying something unreasonable here? Unlike the previous times we are not allowed to discuss anything; in fact, we have to hold our tongues. Upon inquiry, the guards let us know that the Press is also present. Now that's what I call a curious matter. In the middle of taking our test a green light appears on Steve's screen and moments later on my own. We passed the test! What this really means is that our journey can begin. When the realization of having passed our test kicks in I can't hold my emotions any longer. Bursting from joy I slide my chair back, jump up with raised arms and yell a long and loud "Yes!"

At that very moment the unthinkable happens. The Press breaks through the doors, pushing several guards aside. All the while exams of the others are in full swing and officers present are trying to keep the commotion down. Steve and I are in full screen on the CCTV cameras. I receive a high-speed interview, followed by the anchor telling the camera how easy it is for foreigners to get their driver license in China! Can you believe it? The two white guys next to us are completely ignored and have no idea what's going on. Yet neither do we, everything happens in a rush. Thirty minutes later, we stand outside with our brand new semi-legal winnings. We are still flabbergasted when we call Mister Lee to show our gratitude. Of course, as his phone is probably tapped he pretends to know nothing about what happened at the traffic center. Although the tone of his voice reveals a slight pitch higher to the trained ear, thus confirming that he is the brain behind all of this. Even if no one claims the honor, this certainly made our day. I shall never forget it.

New licenses mean new motorcycles. The next day we hook up with Mister Tang, leader of the syndicate. By now, they have grown in number, as we notice when they pick us up. On the back of their motorcycles we are taken to Mister Tang's house. In front of his impoverished apartment, with spray paint on one wall, lies a concrete courtyard. Here and there grass grows out from the cracks – this neighborhood is dusty and dirty. Laundry hangs to dry on dilapidated balconies. Mister Tang urges us to take a drive on his bike, wanting to put us to the test. What he doesn't know is that neither of us ever drove before! Luckily, I know how to shift gear. Well, to be fair I do not, but I guess it must be the same as with an ATV. When I was still working as an outdoor sports instructor we took groups to Belgium to drive in the woods with ATVs. That is the only reference I had, and it turns out that it works exactly the same, thus saving our asses. This does not stop Tang arrogantly looking at my clumsiness and shaking his head.

After this embarrassing display we drive to an industrial area. Chaotic as it may be, motorcycles litter the surplus of low-rise warehouses, as well as repair services, more than you could dream of, not an inch is left untouched. My preference goes out to a tough Chopper. However, a strong dirt bike is highly recommended because of its excellent wheel suspension suitable for the impassable and dangerous roads to come. None other than Mister Tang himself is an expert on this. He is the first man ever to drive from Chengdu to Lhasa. Yes, he had connections and had a sponsor, which meant that a van with spare parts was driving along with him the whole way. Still, for now he is the man! Now we understand why the rest of the gang respects him as they do. We search and test bikes for half a day until we make our choice. Never before have I heard anything about the brand *Jialing*, but I could not care less. Converted for seven hundred US dollars each we purchase brand new dirt bikes! One in blue, the other in red. They come in cardboard boxes and mechanics assemble them in front of our eyes, we are pinching one another to see if it is all real. On account of us being foreigners no one wants to sell us insurance, meaning we have to go about without license plates. The beautiful thing about China is: nobody cares! Splendid. We collect all essentials and some funky full-face helmets.

To show our appreciation to our collaborators we invite them for lunch at a mediocre restaurant. They serve the same shit everywhere anyway. Mister Lee translates a question for his nebulous associate, asking what kind of bikes we drive at home, leaving Steve and I looking at each other with frowned eyebrows. I reluctantly reply that we do not have a bike and come clean that Tang's motorcycle is the first we ever drove. Hearing these words Mister Tang jumps out from his seat, his black beady eyes sparkling from excitement. He yells in poor English with a thick accent: "What? You want to drive to Tibet this way? You are fucking crazy!" Slapping his hand on his bald head, roaring with laughter. From that moment on he lets go of his attitude and is the friendliest man alive. He was initially looking down on us because he thought we were horrible bikers. Now that he knows we are two complete idiots about to embark on the impossible, he gives us mass respect. He consults on what tools to bring and all the ins and outs regarding motorcycle care. Since they are the only ones able to give us a hard time we pay them for their services, still just a nickel and dime in our own currencies. Saying goodbye never felt so good. Now we are free to go wherever we desire.

Our last week in the heart of Chengdu doesn't pass without a struggle, but, overall, we collect wonderful memories. In fact, we move from one thing to the next. For instance, we plant actual trees in the city and enjoy tasty street barbecues, without getting diarrhea. In the marketplace, we find big tubs filled with huge frogs, almost as big as a football – definitely skipping those. Furthermore, they sell pineapple on a stick for nothing, as well as delicious soya snacks and dried fruits. These dried fruits come in a plastic wrapper with the ingredients in both Chinese and English. They often translate things wrong but this one takes the cake. Apparently, dried strips of peach are *sweet potato fucks*. You can't make this up.

Another cool thing is that we are invited by a photographer who was working on a big art project. We have to stand on top of a skyscraper dressed in camouflaged army uniforms with Kalashnikovs in our hands. Guns, grenades, sandbags, fake blood, the whole nine yards. It is somewhat of an honor to participate. As a way to say thank you he takes us to a posh restaurant afterwards. It's kind of a shame that all those gorgeous female models aren't joining. Flirting with one of his cute daughters makes up for it though. Unfortunately, we never got to see the results, but apparently, our dumb faces were exhibited in some Asian museum.

Our hostel in town permanently houses a German beauty who got knocked up by her Tibetan boyfriend, who visits whenever he can. Things are hard for them as he spends a lot of time in prison for the silliest of reasons, receiving blow after blow.

Hearing his heartbreaking story he is undoubtedly innocent, yet corrupt jurisdiction sure knows how to find this guy. Having escaped to Chengdu he is safe for the moment. But doing something as simple as shopping for groceries always leaves him watching his back. He teaches a lot about political issues and the dirty games the Chinese government is playing on the suppressed Tibetan people. Let us not forget their lands were confiscated in cold blood and are still occupied today. While the whole world monitors the Middle Eastern conflict, and seems to have an opinion about that matter, no one bats an eye to the largest Buddhist genocide, and it is grossly ignored.

It is not easy to leave the only place in the world where I am registered with an address. Back home I didn't even have a mailbox or anything, while here, legislation concerning my driver's license forced me to register. In any case I am spared from the horrendous earthquake that would befall this city two years later with an ungraspable number of nearly 70,000 deaths and nearly 20,000 missing. New friendships here became closer than expected. Some give us gifts in the form of Buddhist relics. Others, like the owner of the hostel, give us T-shirts with printed logos from their businesses. He has done so much for us – we wear them gladly. Staff also write encouragements on our new T-shirts with a black marker, and even the cleaning ladies do not let this chance slip by. This special occasion almost moves me to tears. Tibetan friends place a *Khata*, a white silk scarf around our necks and bid us *Tashi Delek* which means good luck; such kind gestures. This small ceremony is performed when, inter alia, dear ones are departing. The free helmets we got when buying our bikes are placed on the wall in the lobby, with our names and signatures written on them. For a moment we feel like true heroes and our journey did not even begin yet.

Time to get some cash before we start the engines. It's approximately a thousand miles to the next big city and another thousand to Lhasa, so we'd better get organized. On the way to the Bank of China, groups of bystanders are being interviewed by a camera crew. We ignore them. I stick my card in the ATM and at that very moment you could hear a pin drop. I turn around to see what was causing the silence, and then I notice everyone watching me, including the camera crew. Seconds later it becomes clear that the machine swallowed my card. Apparently, the exact same thing happened to the group complaining on the street. *Gee, thanks for the heads up!*

According to my receipt money had been drawn but I wonder whether it is gone or will return automatically to my account. With new customers lining up I prevent further calamity by writing DEFECT on my receipt and stick it to the screen with used chewing gum. I cannot help but wonder if I am either very smart or others just plain dumb. Two passing police officers stop to see what the fuss is all about but they ignore my demand for help. Arriving colleagues follow their example, they simply watch while holding their peace. By now, I am losing it and my furious behavior kicks some dents in the aluminum shutter. Standing in the starting block I just want my debit card back, so in frustration I call the owner of the bank in a telephone booth, having successfully wormed out his private telephone number. To the amazement of the police the owner shows up twenty minutes later with the key already in his hand. Due to the new dents, the shutter only opens halfway. The good news is that everyone sees his or her card returned, while receiving the promise that money will be automatically transferred to where it came from.

All this time the cameras have been recording the escalation, unknowingly morphing the situation into epic proportions. When the camera crew draws near for a close-up, the anchor puts her microphone close to my mouth. She then asks me what I think about the bank. In the last hour of my time in the city I immortalize myself. For an exclusive coverage of CCTV I look straight into the camera, raise my middle finger and yell: "Fuck the bank!" Months later it turns out the money did not go back into my account. So I guess I'm the one that got fucked over after all. Well, let them keep it. Perhaps they can fix the shutter I battered.

Start buttons feel the pressure, spark plugs conduct power, engines start running and the exhaust pipes begin to shake. With a group of waving hands that will be sorely missed, our adventure kicks off. Fully packed I have to admit that we are a riding carnival attraction. No matter whom we pass, my mirrors reveal every head turning. These latest models of Jialing draw a lot of attention. New to driving dirt bikes my scrotum is not amused; I assure my travel buddy that I will no longer be able to have kids. Road maps that are not to scale and the absence of traffic signs force us to pause often enough, which is a relief. Occasionally strangers show us the way. Some of them warn us not to stay out at night in this area as local bandits smell tourist wealth from miles away. Due to these serious warnings, we spend our first night in a seedy hotel.

49

Our iron horses are locked away in the garage, saving a lot of time packing in the morning. With the consultations of Mister Tang fresh in our minds we regularly change our oil. Through misty tropical hills, the winding road is getting worse by the hour. Landscapes change from light green rice paddies to valleys with wild rocky rivers, with an insanely strong current. By nightfall, we still hadn't found a suitable spot to set up tent. Pavement has turned its back on us already and driving on these dirt roads in the dark is not exactly our hobby. Passing a slim patch of flatland, possibly the only suitable place around, we cut the cord. Sometimes you have to improvise and sometimes you have to play with the cards you are dealt with; for tonight that means we will be camping along the roadside. At night, the ground literally shakes when lorries drive by, not to mention the noise. Maybe next time we should not roll out the sleeping bags three yards from the traffic.

As the journey continues, I notice I'm going at snail's pace while Steve's motorcycle has plenty of power. After intense examination I find out the break is constantly on due to a misplaced jackscrew. According to Steve that explains why my back light was suspiciously bright. "Would you mind notifying me just a little bit sooner next time?" I say sarcastically, yet in a humorous way. This and other incidents are the harbinger of much more mechanical misfortune to come.

Our third day has a small miracle in store. The hard rain pouring from the heavens makes visibility close to non-existent. Hilly dirt roads in the jungle have turned into sludge, making them hazardous. The absence of a guardrail is not helping our cause either. We want to save money by sleeping in the tent instead of hotels, but today that's simply impossible. Relentless downpour has us soaked to our panties and covered in mud.

When we spot a hotel – the only hotel in the whole wide area as a matter of fact – we take shelter beneath its entrance. The girl of the front desk receives us, and so the bargaining begins. Having gained experience we round it off at a staggering three US dollars a night per person. Is that a business deal or what? Because we are the only guests, we can even park our motorcycles in the lobby. Furthermore, they serve the best lemon-chicken I have possibly ever eaten, and if that isn't enough, by accident we learn we're actually at a location that millions of people covet, *known from TV*, the world-renowned Panda Research Center in Wolan! Pretty much the only place on earth where they legally breed and survey the animals. Had it not been for that rainstorm we would never have known we passed it.

Except for some scattered branches at daybreak, there are no traces of the heavy storm from yesterday. While underway it's noticeable that we are closing in on Tibetan territory. Styles of houses change as well as people's faces and their type of clothing. You have to realize how special this is to us, in a time where no one had heard of YouTube yet, having been launched only a year prior to this. Driving southwest it would be sensible to take Route 318; this is the conventional way to the peaceful nation of the monks. It's nicknamed the *Friendship Highway*, for the simple fact that it is the most travelled route. Via Route 317 there is little chance you'll find aid in case of need, that is if you find a living soul in the first place. That's pretty much all that is known about this northern route, but with hearts of explorers beating in our chests we choose this one, aware of the risks involved. Or so we think.

Going from Xiaojin to Danba we pull over to orientate ourselves. You see, this was well before the age of further developed digital navigation – all we had were road maps and a compass. A man dragging along a donkey shows us the way when we ask for directions. People of this village may have the best soya snacks around, they certainly do not have a sense of direction. Reaching Gouza, close to Kanding, we conclude that the man was just as smart as the animal he was dragging along. We need to make a detour for a few good hours to Xingduqiuo. Realizing this takes us close to Route 318 we begin to wonder if we didn't prematurely judge the talking donkey, perhaps he sent us here on purpose, knowing it would be better for us.

Sometimes we are blessed with pavement, sometimes cursed with sand, and at other times there is gravel, yet always there is an unbelievable amount of dust. My scarf is thoroughly congested with large dust particles, grinding in between teeth and whenever I blow my nose a black goo comes out. Yet we press on. It is heartbreaking to see kids running up the road with hands outstretched begging for money. Ferocious stray dogs are also running up the road but we kick them away to protect ourselves.

Passing the villages of Tagong and Bamei the hills and meadows are green with infinite views. Never before have I seen such awe-inspiring horizons, capable of stretching across such a vast landscape. It is humbling to see how big of a marvellous world we live in. Many years from now I would still enjoy the impression it had left on me. In fact, it is here where I learn how small we are as humans, yet not insignificant. Just before we reach Dawu, mountain slopes are covered in either kaleidoscopic flags or herds of yaks.

We set up camp to save ourselves from the treacherous dark. Having gained much ground in altitude, nights are well below zero degrees. Close-by peaks of the Himalaya range are ready to welcome us. Ice cold streams coming from the slopes are good for fresh drinking water but also for washing our faces, doing the dishes, and for water to boil our supper on cheap camping stoves. During comforting bonfires we eat and enjoy good conversations about God, or no God, women, and issues in our families.

Morning rays are the signal to zip open the tent, and discover a cloudless day with bald eagles circling above. As the sun rises, the earth slowly warms up. Heavy frost has turned our tents white. After breakfast Steve takes a dump across the river while I enjoy the newly-lit fire. I look up as an angel appears from the bushes. It's a young woman, clothed in robes of her tribal heritage and wearing decorative pieces and colorful barrettes in her hair. We stare at each other while she places herself right next to me, not saying a word. I'm sitting face to face with her big black eyes with that typical Asian squint, sculpted cheekbones and flawless hazel skin, elegantly joined by a pink blush. A gentle smile follows. I am lost in her gaze and short of breath when our hands touch. The ceremony only lasts a few minutes before she gets up and vanishes into the nothingness she came from. It ignites a flame of continuing interest in the inspiring culture and nature around. She barely left when Steve returns and finds me with a mysterious glow of inner piece on my face. To this day I do not think he believes my encounter actually took place.

Later that day something else happens that I can hardly believe. Riding into the village of Luhuo Steve appears to have a high fever. Because he's not in a state to drive he strolls into a hotel to ask for help. While I watch over the bikes, I notice him from a distance getting into a car with another man. Without a word, they take off and I am left standing there with a question mark above my head. Observing my surroundings, I watch cows freely roam about, eating whatever they can find. Polluted streets serve rotting food and even a newspaper. They do not seem bothered by the bad menu. A small group of squatted individuals are checking out the engines while others, somewhat resentfully, point out my quality hiking boots.

Six hours pass and still I haven't got a clue what's going on. Surely, I can't leave our stuff unattended, but my worries surpass my patience. Carefully keeping an eye on our belongings, my investigation begins. Asking around for an hour provides the winning answer. An old man sitting on a bench guides me in the direction of a door of a carriage house. Wavering I grab the rusty handle and cautiously open the squeaking door. To my surprise I see my friend on a bed, in a deep sleep with his clothes still on and his head pressed in the pillow as if he is trying to end his life. It is not a spacious room, yet large enough to park the still fully equipped motorcycles between the beds, which I do on the advice from the owner of the carriage house for safety purposes. The sound of the engines causes Steve to awake from his coma, which he falls straight back into after a brief moment of recognition. Having endured a night among heavy petrol fumes it turns out that our friend was in the hospital for a while, and got knocked out by all the medication. Still not knowing what caused the attack he recovers remarkably quickly.

Our last day in the Peoples Republic of China draws closer. Multicolored prayer banners are flapping a welcoming "Hello!" This route has many roads above 5,000 meters, which allows for amazing views as well as headaches and lightheadedness. The surrounding snow is the purest of white. We are wearing double pairs of gloves and pretty much all of the clothing our backpacks have to offer. Obviously, this is where traveling differs from going on holiday. Horrible roads and sharp winds are one thing, driving uphill in second gear only is very frustrating. Thin air at these altitudes just do not provide enough power for the engines. As our journey becomes more intense, our bodyweight reduces hand in hand with the temperature. It takes determination to stay sane. Still I wouldn't want to miss this for the world. A camera duct taped to my handlebar records the harsh conditions. Unsecured steep cliffs, slippery rocks, icy gravel roads and sandy dirt tracks are what we're fighting against. It's a slight comfort that we are not the only ones; semi-truck drivers are facing a similar penury. When passing one another we respectfully wave and smile, as a way to carry the burden together. It's like letting the other one know you understand what he is going through.

Swiftly we transform from clumsy loons to experienced drivers, like taking a crash course. Although one of us takes that a little too literally. Right before I disappear behind a cliff in a curve I check my mirror, only to see my friend sliding over the ever-precarious road. Hastily I return, even quick enough to help him get out from under his motorcycle. Except for disheveled clothes and some bruises he is doing okay. Never get overconfident, this is a lesson well learned. A local Good Samaritan rushes from his nearby hut to aid. With a wet back and iron rod he bends crooked parts back to their original position. After I adjust some mechanical parts we are again, good to go.

Wherever we make a stop to purchase food or go to the bathroom, we are surrounded by interested parties in no time. Taking a picture here or stopping at a gas station there, they flock about in large quantities. In that sense, nothing has changed since we started – still the riding carnival attraction. Judging from their smiles, locals are of a loving nature and genuinely interested. How nice would it be to talk to these people and get to know their thoughts? Surely, we would have participated in a game of pool, as no other country in the world has so many outdoor pool tables. Indeed, a great help against boredom and unemployment too. As of yet verbal communication is impossible – no one speaks even one word of English. So far, we are well received everywhere.

Unfortunately, we can't say the same about where we're heading. Tales of tourists going missing and becoming imprisoned are abundant. We don't have a permit to enter Tibet, nor do we know the exact location of its border. However, as time passes along something appears that might resemble one. Militarized watchtowers on either side of the road, shadowed by a red arch above it. According to our crumpled road map it should be here somewhere.

About a hundred meters in front of the possible border we discuss our options with engines running. The fact that no other vehicles appear to be present in the area greatly increases our chances. From this point on it's uncertain if there are any soldiers in the towers or anyone in wait. Being so close to my long-held dream to enter Tibet I decide to take the initiative and yell: "Follow me!" Engines roaring, I spurt away at full throttle, followed by the Canadian. Abdominal muscles tense up while I hold my breath. From the corner of my eye I detect the left watchtower manned, and filled with anxiety I check my mirror to see if they open fire. So far so good. Riding as fast as we can for a couple of miles we pull over, leaving a trail of dust behind us. By not being chased down or blown to pieces, it dawns on us that we are writing history, because, as of yet, it is undocumented whether anyone else has managed to do this before. Overjoyed at our accomplishment we celebrate our successful journey. It is hard to believe that we really made it to these raw forbidden lands, hidden from the public. Our hearts overflow with solemnness.

It is a peculiar thing to feel so at home in a place you've never been before. With the absence of a permit nor any official authorization, this is how we enter into Tibet, a sacred country, known and admired since ancient times as the Roof of the World.

4

TIBET

For some reason the majority of people picture Tibet as a place with rocks, snow and ice, and not much else. This cannot be further from the truth. Perpetual flatlands, solid pine forests, green rice fields and barren deserts, you name it. Everything is here and it is nothing less than breathtaking.

Close to Jomda one can't help but notice the paradox of the beautiful nature. Concrete and steel is going through the roof, humongous ugly construction sites wherever you place your eye. They are building tunnels and dams as if it were paper-mâché. Also hundreds of miles of roadwork. *Just what is going on here?* All this time the amount of asphyxiating dust in the air has not diminished, it is simply inexpressible if you have not experienced it for yourself. Disarrayed, we long for a shower, it is not exactly an excessive luxury given we have not bathed for a week. Tonight's place to crash also denies us the opportunity. Yet we cannot complain; we get a room with two beds for ten yuan, which is but one US dollar. Surrounded by poverty it feels awkward at times to spend without limit. In spite of the low prices we are almost out of cash.

Riding into the city of Qamdo, also known as Chamdo, which to our limited knowledge is being pronounced as Changdu, we drove our first thousand miles and just spent our last pennies on a tasteless meal and gasoline. Then the hunt for a much-desired ATM starts. Local banks, nameless banks, the Agricultural Bank, we spot all of them. We visited a total of seven in this fifth largest city and no Bank of China. Steve has Canadian dollars and Traveller Cheques, I have euros and US dollars. When none of the banks are willing to exchange our money a rare occurrence takes place that could have ended a lot worse. We are relatively young and haven't yet learned to control ourselves.

The idea of not having any money makes our already frustrated minds totally desperate. So we snap. My friend kicks the front desk shouting: "What kind of bank are you? Change the goddamn money!" While I am discussing options with the manager, the employees call headquarters to see if they are allowed to provide a onetime exception. We find out that during this first week of May, the country has a national holiday. Nobody answers the phone in Beijing, so no exceptions are granted. Now patience has left the building. We refuse to leave without being served, even as the last customers close the door behind them and guards already lower the shutters. We do not have any elaborate plans, but the next step comes so in sync that it seems we can just read each other's minds.

Steve pushes a guard aside and sees chance to open the shutters. I run outside and jump on my motorcycle to park it behind the gate of the bank. Behind a small bulge, I get the shock of my life when a uniformed man grabs his Uzi! I am still not a fan of machine guns, especially when they are pointed at me! *Okay better not here*, I think to myself. Fortunately, he does not chase me, or worse. Probably deluded by the shock I decide to park in the bank itself, I do not claim that my actions make any sense here. Arriving at the front of the building, Steve is still struggling with the guard. Full throttle I bounce up the three steps at the entrance and pulling the break I park with a 90-degree angle and squeaking tires that actually leave a mark on the large floor tiles of imitation marble. Rubbery smells arise. Steve throws me his keys and quickly I jump on his motorcycle too. Bouncing up the steps, I feel like Tom Cruise as I have to duck due to the shutters already lowering again. By the time I park the second bike, the shutters are sealed shut and we find ourselves locked inside. An ill-considered choice for people already illegal in the region. The manager yells while he seems both angry and afraid at the same time. Considering that he is coming from such a different culture, we both have this feeling in common.

Wound up as we are, we mean business though. About an hour of heavy negotiations pass by, now we're more or less waiting to get arrested. They probably just keep us talking until the police arrives to handcuff us and carry us away, never to be seen again.

Then a remarkable thing happens. The police does get involved, however not in the manner you might expect. Somewhere in a nearby university, two English students were apprehended by the officers and escorted to the bank. Well what do you know? They deliver us our own translators! Hats off for the students who are trying to pull some serious strings but just like our attempts, it ends unsuccessfully. Hours later we are outside again, sitting on the sidewalk having failed miserably with zero money in our pockets, yet by a miracle we are still grateful for our freedom and our lives. What the hell were we thinking?

With the sun already resting behind the mountains, the temperature is dropping fast. Shaking off the city's dust, we leave the rest of the journey to chance, staying here will only be counterproductive. In the next thousand miles we'll have to press our luck. Troubled thoughts eclipse the scenic view on snowy peaks. We have convinced ourselves that the bending dirt roads most likely take us towards a certain death. Nothing can be further from the truth. Truly, somebody from above must be watching over us. A group of youth is blocking the road ahead, yet upon inspection, they start decorating our bikes with fresh flowers. If that isn't crazy enough they bless us with a plastic bag filled with food, which we gladly receive. What are the chances of that happening when we needed it most? There is also meat inside that does not require a refrigerator; it simply won't go bad at these altitudes.

Driving for a few hours the hands of time reach midnight. By now, it's so cold that we are literally emptying our backpacks on the lane, in search of more clothes to wear. Millions of stars are twinkling down upon us, showing the way where inconsistent roadmaps fail. The moonlight is bright enough to light up surrounding summits, even in the far distance, no photo could capture the splendor but the view remains immortalized in my memory. Meanwhile the roads begin to freeze, making it dangerous to drive.

For a while already we are on the lookout for a decent place to sleep, yet nothing presents itself. Climbing in low gear, we pull over on the top of a large hill, shivering uncontrollably. Close-by houses from yak manure and straw give us hope, it is always better to set up camp near any type of civilization. Strong winds make it nearly impossible to get the tents erected, they are not even up for ten minutes and it already starts to snow – adding fire to the fuel so to speak. We are too tired to eat but too hungry to sleep. Do you know that feeling? Knowing myself, sleep will flee on an empty stomach so I make a fire and we enjoy the food from the plastic bag given to us. Somehow free food tastes better too. When my eyelids finally close, they stay that way until the very morning. Exhaustion is beginning to embrace us. While I'm entangled in this epic campaign in the middle of nowhere I think of back home, where today they are celebrating Liberation Day.

Morning light reveals a white Shangri-La. A thick blanket of snow has changed the scenery completely; as far as the eye can see there are colossal mountains all around. Our own tents have turned into miniature snowy mountains, covered in only one night. From one of the nearby huts a girl shows herself and to our surprise she beckons us to come over. Without thinking twice, we drop whatever we have in our hands and blindly follow her into the hut, where things are cozy and warm with a fireplace going on. A framed picture of a young Dalai Lama decorates the mantelpiece. This area is so removed from modern society that I wonder whether they are aware that he is an old man now. Another girl enters the house. Steve and I look at each other and get all kinds of wholly inappropriate fantasies. That dream immediately goes down the drain when the girl pulls a few-weeks-old baby from beneath a pile of blankets that is lying next to me on a wooden bench. "Good thing I didn't sit there!" I lark about. When we seek permission to take pictures, they shyly refuse at first. Thirty minutes later, when they are adorned in traditional robes and odd-looking jewelry in their hair, they are ready to be eternalized. In this day and age where we take photography for granted, due to our abundance of technology, it still holds meaning to them. In fact, they take great pride in it. We are almost moved to tears to see them making such an effort. Another example of how the West with striving progressiveness assassinated romance. Sometimes I really wonder if I was born like five generations too late.

Asking whether we are hungry they serve us white bowls with dry flower. Impatient as we are we take a spoon, directly coughing a cloud of flower as a result. The girls make fun of us and rightly so. To complete the meal, they pour something best described as a brown goo in our bowls. We have heard tales about this local delicacy; it has to be yak butter tea. A solid lump of butter is added as a finishing touch. My whole body rejects it from the first mouthful, yet regardless how disgusting it is, I keep on eating in order not to offend the girls' culture. Ten minutes pass before I have to excuse myself. Drinking hot melted butter on a more or less empty stomach is not a good idea. Hastily I look for a hidden place in the open fields. Even before I find a private spot, I vomit half of it out, and the other half sprays out of my behind with pants down my ankles. Close call. Thanks to the alarming noises in my bowels I am just in time to unbuckle my pants. This is how I donate it back to nature – undoubtedly the most atrocious thing I ever ate. After this minor incident, we thank them for their hospitality and go our way. Other residents of the mini village have woken up by now, their curiosity along with them. Though helping us to pack our stuff is well intended, they do more damage than good. Not being familiar with the equipment they cause everything to be twisted and crooked.

Growing in life experiences, we almost forget that we are completely broke. The only reason we are able to drive our dirt bikes is because of the compassion from passers-by, willing to fill up our tanks with gasoline for free. If it were not for this unprecedented kindness, we would probably be stranded. Meanwhile we switched to the Friendship Highway for our own benefit and luckily our decision is paying off. This road honors its name due to the saviors providing the necessary aid. With the jerry can filled we are good to go, except for our bellies that remain empty. What is left of our rations consists of biscuits and dry noodles. At one point, we're almost getting used to it. Standard free tea everywhere has us stop frequently at road side cafeterias, at least in populated areas. In the more remote ones we survive by drinking from creeks and puddles.

On one of these challenging nights we are exhausted to the core. We do not even bother to set up the tents and only roll out our sleeping bags. Our wish to sleep in until daybreak is not granted because a group of kids has spotted these two white devils. Shy but on guard, they close in on us. With their tiny backpacks and adorable crimson cheeks, they are huggable. All of them make a poor and dirty impression. Unfortunately we have nothing to give them except for a handshake and smile, and who knows, perhaps for the moment that is enough. When a large truck passes, they suddenly start chasing it, shouting their little lungs out. As it heeds to the sharp voices and slows down, they open the tailgate to climb in while giving each other a hand and count themselves lucky. Today they won't have to walk all the way to school.

Random Jeeps spoil us once more with free gasoline and we saddle up. Our Chinese motorcycles are nothing less than cool looking, but nothing more either. Every other day they break down. Having to tighten the chain is a continuing issue, bits and pieces are held together by duct tape, and when my exhaust pipe starts making an awful sound we find some bolts rattled out, the beginning of sorrows. To our advantage, no matter how small a village, no matter how remote, there are always at least twenty mechanics around – or people presenting themselves as such.

All this time the chilly breezes are acceptable due to the warmth of the intense sun. Confiner forests have the sweetest aromas almost putting us into a trance. All that green, accompanied by the marvellous sight of herds of yaks grazing the steppe grass, where it is not uncommon to spot wild horses mingle among them. The continent of Asia at its finest. After gaining miles we make progress, occasionally driving through rivers and over conspicuous suspension bridges, which can be nerve wrecking. To say we are defying death is an exaggeration, but I bet other people would beg to differ. Odometers turn overtime when motion comes to a sudden halt. Sandy dirt roads are offended by my incursion, my intrusion leads me to be thrown out of balance, perhaps a revenge from the sandy roads for having disturbed their everlasting lonesomeness. I guess it was always inevitable – I come to fall! Thanks to my moderate speed and a little bit of luck there is no harm done. Not this time.

When hostile roads finally intersperse to pavement we are held from gaining serious miles. A string of traffic blocks both lanes. Driving in between cars and trucks we make it to the front, wondering what the deal is. Policemen are raising hands signaling us to stop. As if we could drive on if we wanted to as heavy roadworks are in full progress. Huge machines are tarmacking new lanes. Our young lives have so much to learn still as it only takes half an hour for us to grow impatient. I spot a narrow access next to the yellow machines and a steep embankment. Covertly I consult Steve about the opportune dilemma – not without risk. It does not take long before boldness overtakes our stirred, eager hearts. The handlebar being the widest item I turn my left mirror inside, increasing my space. When starting the engines, the bystanders assume that we will turn around. Well-trained officers however are watching every move we make, yet in spite of their attentiveness they can't prevent what happens next. We're back at pushing our luck to the limit. My heart pounding in my chest I go full throttle through the narrow access, alongside the steamy machine that will finish me instantly may it swerve. Seeing that it works out, my friend gives gas until he's on my tail. Police are running back and forth, frustrated for they are beaten, standing empty handed with no chance of chasing the escaped convicts. Their cars are too heavy for the soft tarmac anyway. Our motorcycles are light enough to soar above the soft road surface. There we go, driving as the first ones ever on a brand-new paved road in rural Tibet! With no fear of getting caught either as for weeks roadworks have been terrorizing the neighborhood, which is why we have not met a soul for dozens of kilometers.

When finally we do meet a soul, it is the beautiful one of a woman named Wei. She is willing to exchange our foreign money into local currency, saving our asses. When we run into her later that day, she even buys us dinner. Most people would not do this for their own family, yet she chooses to trust these two strangers. People like her make the world go round. At least, if it actually was, but you get the point.

Snow has turned into ice, everything is frozen. Only the sun makes the bitterness humane. Strings of *Lung Ta's* flap in the strong winds, often attached to Buddhist shrines, the white stupas majestic in their element. Square prayer flags in blue, yellow and red are called *wind horses*. When seeing their glory you know that you have accomplished something. A few high-passes above the five thousand meters mark, the altitude attacks us in full armor. It frustrates me to the bone that our engines just cannot get enough power due to the altitude. Steadily the rocky mountains give way to colossal sand dunes mixed with dark and light colors.

Passing the last ridge a huge anomaly appears in the hazy distance. Our helmets removed and engines turned off we gaze at the mirage in the valley. Checking the road map we don't find any evidence of the massive blueprint the desert presents us. Descending the hills until we make it to the edge, our jaws drop. This is no ordinary city: high construction, big apartments, factories, houses and complete shopping malls, no windows and all grey from concrete. Everything is just thrown up! Streets are empty, not even a single vehicle around, and not a soul in a city which could hold tens of thousands, more likely a hundred thousand. I am shocked. Driving through silent blocks sends shivers down my spine.

Can the rumors be true? I've heard them speak about projects of unbelievable proportions, namely forty-seven new airports, endless tunnel systems, underground bunkers, twelve new dams the size of the Hoover Dam and eleven new cities such as the one we are baffled by at this very moment. In two years' time the entire country is being renovated. This will be China's big chance to show competing nations that they are no longer a third world country. The insane amount of workforce to be summoned, better yet slave labor, is unsurpassed. In all the craziness of the ghost town, we actually come across a previously much needed Bank of China. Peering through the windows, we spot an ATM still wrapped up. The question remains, who is going to populate this city?

A mere sixty kilometers away from our destination and the fulfilment of a boy's dream, the struggle continues. My bike throws the towel in. Really? Is this the right moment for mechanical failure? Instinctively we check the gasoline and change the spark plug. This is not my day. Even the stickers I placed on my handlebar, reading *lucky seven*, have turned their backs on me. Out of pure vexation I throw my helmet to the ground and kick my bike repeatedly, as we have done many times in the past weeks. This causes several items to bend.

During one of the helmet-throwing incidents, it accidentally changes direction and we actually have to hike a small valley to recover it. At last, we discover a jackscrew missing from the kickstand. Just so you know, these models are fitted with a mechanism that when you pull the kickstand out, the engine automatically shuts off. Now the system thinks it is out while still in. Of course, the jackscrew is nowhere to be found. As a temporary solution I twist another screw out of a random place that I think I won't be needing. Let's hope I'm right.

Before reaching the capital we are to face our final enemy: a beast of an approaching sandstorm. Intolerable hoary deserts bring forth violent winds with a mixture of dry sand and rain, which are somehow not intermingling. Nonetheless, it is a powerful demon devouring anything in its way. Not knowing the strength and anger of the dark storm we don't seek shelter, not that there is any. Charging from the side I can barely get a grip on the handlebar. Gusts of wind make us tilt siding against it, whilst we try our best not to fall. We are literally hanging in there, no pun intended. By the time our motorcycles drive straight the monster is behind us. We snap pictures and are relieved that we are still alive to see another day. The universe accommodates us with new pavement to enjoy, probably as compensation. As we are the only ones around we drive side by side. While we are both accelerating, my blood starts coursing rapidly through my veins. Surely not without reason, the view through inanimate trees announces the finish line. Excitement has us cheering and laughing, arms raised in midair.

With the last clouds dissolving the stomach butterflies increase. The feeling can best be compared with being in love, or worthy of reward, a victor even. Bright light from above illuminates the sacred hill with beguiling white walls and lofty burgundy rooftops, little square windows and huge banners. There she is in all her glory, the cradle of mystical wisdom: the Potala Palace! Without any form of coordination, we race through the city toward our bounty which is elevated above all else. Bumping up the sidewalk, we park straight in front of the awe-inspiring structure. We jump up and down, we hug and repeatedly shout: "We made it!" Passers-by take pictures of us and we ask them if they're willing to do the same with our own cameras. Conveniently looking away, I prevent people from seeing some tears of release and happiness roll down my cheeks. This voyage of privations counts three thousand kilometers so far, from Chengdu to Lhasa, almost all of it off-road. Straight through an area of which its very existence is being disputed. Except for Mister Tang, at present we are the only ones in the world who have managed to do this. After not having showered for a while we are smelly, hairy, feral and repulsive, yet overjoyed in our hearts. With the help of other vehicles, I travelled about twenty thousand kilometers overland. Quite the accomplishment. We did the impossible and proved the scoffers wrong. In the last weeks Jeffrey Vonk and Stephen Nagy wrote history, up until the final day.

China, including the stolen province of Tibet, is the country where they eat rice with chop sticks, where children walk about without pants so they can shit wherever they please – which they do by the way – and where girls who reckon themselves artists perform half naked at kids shows. It is also the country where they eat anything with a pulse, where you are not allowed to stop during a traffic accident to help your fellow compatriot, and where burping, slurping and smacking during eating is accepted as normal.

Lhasa is built in a valley of the mighty Himalayan range on a height of well over three and a half kilometers. Not too high, but it *is* for someone living most of his life beneath sea level. While panting for breath with a pounding headache we finally arrive at a hostel. Having a bathroom is a delight. Sure, the toilet itself is still just a hole in the floor, but having a door is nice for a change. By now, we are almost accustomed to public toilets, often shared. Imagine doing number two, squatting down above a hole with no dividers allowing you some privacy. Apparently, it is very intriguing to watch a white dude taking a crap.

While my travel buddy is bed bound with a serious flu, I roam ancient squares and streets where monks in blood red robes are begging, whilst drumming their silver prayer wheels. Vendors sell delicious momos at simple stands, small shrines have different fragrances of incense burning. Visiting the Potala Palace I conclude it was worth everything to come here. An airplane may have been faster but it cannot be compared to the sheer happiness of having completed a journey. Dark carpets with white inscriptions decorate the facades. Golden buddhas intrigue with piercing brows, as well as the timeworn tapestries with embroidered legendary sagas. Bald-shaved monks turn the long rows of copper prayer mills on the westside of the complex, making them spin around to, spiritually speaking, throw the mantras into the world. A religious custom that has been practiced daily for centuries. Locals make entry for the price of a symbolic one yuan, while westerners pay a hundredfold. Still you don't hear me complain. It truly is a privilege to stand here where the gods themselves were once present. And all of this on May 14, my birthday. Today I turn twenty-six.

One cannot help noticing swastikas all around the place. Painted on walls outside, printed on cars, carved into furniture and even carved into the skin of the elderly. Locals seem completely ignorant to the fact that an evil man from the 1930s borrowed the Buddhist sign for purposes known. Questioning people about the Second World War results in the revelation that pretty much none of them had done their homework. One proper lesson to be learned here, the government controls exactly what the people are allowed to know and not know. To their credit, in the West we are not exactly taught about their history either, which contain an endless number of dynasties.

One thing is for sure, the Chinese have utterly pillaged Tibetan culture. The once so peaceful monk village of Zhöl has turned into an enormous city thanks to the atheist oppressors, spreading like locusts. They certainly do know how to get rid of nostalgia.

Summiting a mountain ten miles from this regional capital treats me to a view of the entire valley plus the encompassing white peaks as far as the eye can see. Having spent the night in my single tent on the edge of a cliff, crampons prevent me from sliding on the way down, going all the way through a steep canyon. When snow in my sports bottle melts, I use it for drinking water. Without anything to eat, I make it back to the foot of the mountain, drained from energy and with a sunburned face. Two hours pass before a utility truck comes by with blocks of rock in the open back which have been blown out of the hills with dynamite. The previous day I actually heard the sound of the explosions echo through the concatenations of valleys.

Hitchhiking along we end up somewhat close to the hostel where Steve is still recovering. At the property where the truck unloads those rocks I see something that makes me unpalatably sad. Power tools hack them to small pieces and once more into even smaller pieces, until they can be worked with hammer and chisel, tools held by the hands of children. Groups of preteens are working these stones under poor conditions, only to answer the growing demand of hard stone in the wealthy West. Condemned to modern-day slavery and no one gives a flying fuck. That is the world we live in today. As long as we get to buy our favorite products at the garden center we don't care how it got there, or who had to suffer for it.

Due to the many mechanics around, we have our bikes totally refurbished. Pretty much every single item has to be fixed or replaced. That is the price you pay for a *Made in China*.

Anyway, we are good to go for our next road trip. We move north for the weekend to the heavenly lake of Namtso. On an altitude of four thousand seven hundred meters lies the highest salt water lake in the world. At least, that is what it is famous for. Heading towards it, a van cuts me off by switching lanes without a signal light or any notice at all. I have to pull the breaks so hard my motorcycle loses balance and I nearly come to fall. Not a boy, but perhaps not a man yet either I kick a dent in his door and while driving next to the van I raise my middle finger and yell: "Fuck you asshole!" Some biker behavior eh? Not saying I am proud of those actions.

Having left the crowdedness of the city behind, the mesmerizing infinite plains await us; yellow grasslands stretching from here to the horizon. In the distance, we marvel at another rumor that turns out to be true. With our own eyes we see what newspapers boast about. The forsaken yet spotless territory is cut in half by the construction of a brand-new railway line. So the reports of the thousands of miles long iron serpent were trustworthy. Now we witness what nobody ever expected, all to serve the explosion of tourists that shall flood the nation in two years' time.

A fading mountain range ahead notifies us that we missed a turn somewhere and took the wrong way. Returning to where we came from and hours upon hours later we finally guess the right direction. Spotting a rusty arch looping over the road, our doubts are removed. A red-white roadway gate bar and guarded tollbooth herald the entrance of Namtso Natural Reserve Park. I am not a fan of paying for something that nature offers for free, but if you wish to see some things of this world, you have to abide to the rules sometimes. Above five thousand meters a sheer visual sensation unfolds. The lake is a retina triggering wonder, a coalition of the divine and mortal, a masterpiece of the Creator himself. Turquoise waters stir the senses, the purest of ice resting at its shores. Descendants of ancient tribes have pitched their tents here and built suitable huts from yak manure. By sound of approaching engines, the children run to the side of the road and wave hello. Their delighted facial expressions when we wave back melt my heart.

Early the next day everything smells like our rented yurt, having me too excited to sleep in. Pairs of black-necked cranes soar the water surface as yaks chew the grass, some brown, some white, but all undisturbed by never ceasing sharp winds.

Oral traditions have us believe that the lake is holy for the surrounding tribes. No one is allowed to set sail, swim or quench their thirst in it. When no one is watching, I reckon it is time to put the myth to the test. I fill my cup and take a sip, and another one, and another. When Steve tastes it he comments that the water is nothing remotely close to salty. He smiles from ear to ear saying: "So fresh!" A nearby Chinese couple is appalled by my action, yet eager to test for themselves upon hearing the results. This ain't the highest salt water lake in the world as their Lonely Planet travel guidebook states. By all means it is sweeter than sweet. Conspiracies are quickly drawn. Upon certain invasion in time of war, this lake is the biggest fresh water supply in the world, no enemy will seek to contaminate water that is supposed to be undrinkable. It is a treasure of a reservoir, and none are aware of it except the elite and those within the highest levels of government. It seems like one of their dirty little secrets is now being exposed. Blown away by the number of fully staffed military bases along the way, which probably is the reason behind the banning of tourism in the area, a saying by Napoleon Bonaparte comes to mind. He said: "China? There lies a sleeping giant. Let him sleep, for when he awakes he will move the world." Now that the red dragon slowly shakes the dust from its feet, it might prove the little French warlord to be correct.

Filming the perimeter, I boldly walk among dwelling places. A young woman sticks her head out of one of the hairy tents, more or less inviting me for tea. Without hesitation I crawl in through a slender opening behind a flap. Her child is scared to death when he lays eyes upon the white devil. Inside is another woman who couldn't care less about openly breastfeeding her newborn. Now that I have been without the touch of the opposite sex for so long, it actually turns me on a little bit. Trying to communicate turns out to be quite a challenge. Smells of the fire in the center of the tent are excruciating –

if you could only smell dried burning yak shit... A unit of molecules nests in nose hairs where they feel safe and decide to reside for the next few hours.

Fleeing the scene, I meet up with Steve who is already packing. It seems like we have to flee from something else. A cirrocumulus is rolling our way, and I don't recall ever having seen such a threatening dark cloud. One of nature's dazzling wonders, yet a deadly one, is heading straight towards us. Even the geo-engineered storms of today would be ashamed of this massive tyrant. Tribespeople hasten to their homes – being able to read the sky they know what is upon us.

Naively thinking that we will outride the cloud, it catches up with us in record speed. Our route leads partly toward the front of this heavenly army, about to unleash the battle, hence resolving to go off road. Skeletons of yaks and sheep are scattered across bumpy lands. Driving as fast as we possibly can, in a last attempt to escape the horrors, appears to be not fast enough. Raging winds carrying hail and snow attack in full force. It hurts our poorly covered faces. Within no time the landscape turns white, eliminating any view of direction. Blessed with the sense of direction of carrier pigeons we hit asphalt again not long after.

The torturous weather conditions continue until the cloud bends south. The damage already done, patches of snow swiftly freeze to ice, on our bikes as well as on our faces. Riding back up the high-pass we are as slow as ever, shivering from the cold. Lacking the necessary outfit, the cold soon turns into hypothermia. Then an intense downpour leaves us drenched, my legs are all wet as my ski pants are far from waterproof, Steve's arms are all wet from wearing a winter coat, also not waterproof. Omitting summits of the white mountains donate temperatures that could turn a North Alaskan resident cranky. You have to realize, even when you have to pee there is no way to open your pants with frozen fingers, let alone grab your phallus. Descending the other side on dangerous rocky trails, the infuriated weather gods turn their faces against us. After filling up the bikes at

China Petrol, the dominating petrol supplier, it starts to dribble again. Rather quickly, this whirls into a rainstorm that drowns us, erasing all sight with a thick curtain of water, flooding the road with three inches. All the while obliterating winds overpower me until I scream aloud from agonizing pain, having developed serious hypothermia in my knees and fingers. My legs are literally unable to stretch and the senses have long left my fingers, due to having drenched gloves. Only pain remains. Steve faces similar challenges. Diligently we search for cover, a shack for shelter or anything to save us from possible death. We would not be the first lives claimed by the barren tundra.

Disesteeming the powers of nature itself, I suddenly spot a tiny tunnel on the left. I lower my speed until my buddy has a visual. I cannot pull over in fear of falling with legs that possibly won't stretch. Seeking refuge I drop with my shoulder against the concrete wall. It is all I can do with a body that can't move. Moments later we are standing there together. Repeatedly my friend mumbles in a soft shaky voice: "I'm so cold." His mumbling sounds like repetitive prayers. We are both in shock. With pinched eyes from the pain I make an effort to walk, but fail immediately. While the hostile curtain of disaster was sagging away we spot a low building across the lanes. Our last hope switched to survival mode we crawl towards it before the night sets in. Miraculously we find it staffed. *Goodness gracious we are saved!* About ten men fill the damp house. They are very surprised to see us. Due to their hospitality, we can dry our clothes near the wood stove and warm ourselves. They serve us herbal tea, noodles and a soup with large chunks of yak meat in a tin can. We eat quickly before they change their minds, starved as we are. Thankfully while sitting and communicating among the men our body joints slowly start to defrost. We find out that these seven beds that are crammed next to one another without any walking space is their mobile home, their temporary living room if you will. Yes, that is right, seven beds for at least ten men. Here are the hardworking laborers that are building the railway track to Lhasa, the first in its kind. We are grateful for their kindness and are forever in debt to these heroes. Who knows what could have happened had it not been for them?

Xigaze or Shigaze is the second largest city of Tibet. Skidding through its dirty streets we are struck by the sheer number of outdoor sport stores. The locals thrive on the swarms of climbers. Unpaved roads are hazardous, mud and rocks give us a hard time. In fact one of these rocks proves to be too much of a challenge. For the second time I come to fall. My brake pedal is all bent, unfortunately due to my own ankle that is stuck beneath it. Turning blue, it swells up instantly. Being far from comfortable the painful journey continues.

Days pass on tracks with heavy roadwork until we reach the highest summit so far, five thousand five hundred fifty-two meters! We pitch our tents among strings of hundreds of colorful prayer flags that are flapping in the wind – you have to see it to believe it; the sight will make any travelers' heart skip a beat. Once again they are accompanied by an indispensable white stupa, symbolizing the ancientness of their teachings of wisdom and worship.

With the sunset comes the increasing cold, by now we are wearing everything we have. The high altitude robs me of my much-needed sleep, turning me into a zombie. Morning light reveals black circles around my eyes and skin evidently turning grey. Shortage of oxygen is good for nobody. In the afternoon, the next road sign greatly lifts our spirits. It's so exciting to be closing in on yet another dream that is about to be turned into reality.

Before us lies the entrance to a park so large that it is easily as big as an entire country. Praised for its unprecedented biodiversity, of course, I am speaking about the Qomolangma National Nature Preserve. Known by Tibetans as the region that hosts the Holy Mother, the tallest mountain in the world, better known as the Mount Everest.

Leaving the first check post behind the view is phenomenal. Rust-colored mountains writhe as if molded by a force powerful beyond measure. A surplus of sea shells and petrified sea creatures are but echoes of our occult distant past. Even on these incredible heights, there is little doubt that all of this was once at the mercy of a submerged event, exactly as several ancient accounts describe. Dare I say the Great Flood?

At least once a day we need to pull over when something breaks in one of the bikes. Zip-tights, duct tape and wire are holding the parts all together. New prayer flags greet us at the last high-pass before the last ninety kilometers toward our destination. Crowned by blue skies and cheerful sunshine a living painting unfolds. Right in front of us, from the left side of the horizon to the right a sequence of the tallest snow-capped mountaintops, the entire awe-inspiring Himalaya Range! No photograph can remotely resemble what our eyes are staring at, no words can describe the sublime perfection. Truly, this is the Roof of the World! Overtaken by sudden emotions due to this astounding natural beauty we flop down and cry, both remaining silent. Ever since I was a toddler and heard the term *eternal snow* for the first time this picture was on my mind. Without a shadow of a doubt the most impressive thing I have ever seen. Not so much for a group of Japanese tourists arriving at the scene in Jeeps. They seem more interested in two white backpackers than in the view, insolent snapping away at our contemplating faces.

At nighttime, the meals in a rancid guesthouse leave nothing to boast over. At least we have some distraction from girls who work in the restaurant, since we're the only guests. While they are braiding Steve's hair and stroking mine, they stick out their tongues. We were assuming that they thought we smelled bad or something but the owner later explains that it's a Tibetan custom. Whenever someone likes you this is their way of showing it. When we understand the custom, it unleashes a groove of sticking out our tongues to pretty much every girl we come across, with flirtatious yet funny moments to follow. Tomorrow is the big day so we wisely hit the sack early, thus receiving the gift of a real bed one last time. We smuggle in a female guest but don't get your hopes up, it is a hungry puppy, enjoying the warmth of the tip of my smelly blanket.

Supposedly, we are not allowed any further with our bikes. Due to the protected Nature Preserve, we are ordered to take an environmentally friendly bus. When the deteriorated diesel arrives, we know that this is a freaking scam. Traversing the rough depleted terrain on roads from cut-away rocks, the excitement builds and we forget about our minor misunderstanding.

Stepping out at Rongbuk Monastery we are mere miles away from Base Camp. Typical architecture with white ramparts and golden shrines makes time stand still, as if nothing changed since 1902 when it was erected. Sounds of little tinkling bells give away that horses are approaching, beautifully ordained like all the cattle around. When clouds are fading the triangular summit of Everest looks proud and dignified. Walking towards it we are picked up by truck drivers that are kind enough to give us a lift. Sitting on the back in between the rubble really provides a sense of the joy of wandering this earth.

It's easy to find a place to sleep in one of the traditional Tibetan tents, however, that's not what I travelled half the world for. The plan is to set up camp at the foot of the mountain, but the entrance to Base Camp is sealed off to those without a Climbing Permit. It's not like we have forty thousand US dollars in an old sock, which is the average cost of going up. Therefore, we forge a sinister masterplan, ready to be executed by nightfall when security is low. Sneaking up on the barrier to enter without being seen is an instant failure. A man in charge of regulation spots us and questions our presence at this unusual hour. We come up with a lie stating that we are here to re-supply one of the current expeditions. Only a few weeks ago I was emailing Harry Kikstra, a Dutch climber and the owner of Seven Summits. While he replied that he was already in Camp 3, I informed him we were on our way. Mentioning his name persuades the guard to let us in. It worked!

Jubilant of our achievement we begin to discuss how we will climb this baby illegally. Our good mood soon turns into sorrow though. People at Base Camp are exceedingly sad and defeated. The late spring of 2006 would be marked by the season with the most deaths, seventeen in total. Because of excellent weather conditions too many risks are taken by too many inexperienced and experienced climbers alike. Teammates of the fallen are spread out with their heads in their hands. Furthermore, through walkie-talkies the coordinators of a certain expedition connect a lost climber to his wife back home, to whom he is saying his last words to. This man ended up somewhere on Everest in an undisclosed location; undoubtedly death will set in soon enough. It is an unrealistic and emotional moment, and a harsh reality-check that this is no game.

Out of respect we set up our tents with a relative distance from theirs. Doing so with a light breeze and falling snow. I hope that things will change for the better tomorrow.

The misty morning hours shows the silhouette of a guy at one of the nearby tents – time for a little chitchat. My eyebrows rise when we find out this two-meter tall beefcake is only fifteen years of age! The blond Australian desired to summit Everest as the youngest person ever. This morning he returned without standing there. Disappointed by his failure, he sighs with a certain relief in his voice: "Well, at least I'm still alive." Right he is. The adolescent daredevil hired a complete camera crew and writer to document his adventure. He continues, "Half of my crew is missing and yesterday the writer sadly lost his life." We reply: "Is his name Lincoln Hall?" The boy wonders how and where we got this information. His face becomes pale when we explain to him that we overheard him say goodbye to his loved ones. This is the gruesomeness of Alpinism. Going our separate ways, we wish him well and set mind to matter. After all, we have our own things to worry about.

Climbing with terrible headaches, fever and a bruised ankle is one thing, going up without oxygen cylinders will become a guaranteed problem. Moreover, we do not have time to acclimatize before our rations run out, so I guess it is a race against the clock. Making preparations we are granted a sack of apples by a Russian climber. The poor guy has no face anymore; absence of such a simple thing as sunscreen has strands of skin hanging down his head, utterly burned by the insane bright sunlight reflecting from off the snow. Concrete boxes acting as bathrooms are atrocious by sight and smell. Six feet deep holes are filled up to the edge with shit, and more. Feasting upon the human waste it truly is a paradise for the flies. Equipped with instructions from skilled people in the camp and coupled with our own experience, our under-qualified ascension begins.

With ground level already at seventeen thousand feet we're gasping for breath. Every step we take the body rejects, a feeling known to me from other climbs. A rotting yak corpse produces odors that make you want to puke, even from a distance, the stench is intolerable. It probably succumbed to exhaustion by carrying heavy loads. Herds of the animals are used to re-supply expedition camps, led by Sherpas. Via a returning group we find out that Camp 2 is beyond today's reach, and you will not have a summit view going up. Acknowledging the fact that we are poorly trained we try our luck on the opposite site. Hiking next to Rongbuk Glacier a large rock stands out with the appearance of an altar from former times. Always remaining youthful in nature, I strip naked and pose on the rock despite of the freezing cold, with Everest in the background. Steve is making sure the moment is memorialized on camera. The timing is perfect, by the time I'm tying my shoelaces a handful of Sherpas arrive with a herd of yaks. The glacier itself stands glorious. Thirty feet tall columns of blue ice are shoulder to shoulder, a frozen army of giants, lost in time. The unspoiled elegance holds mystical energies in this unexplored vastness. Days pass until we stumble upon an unknown camp, toward the route of the West Ridge, for those planning to take the French Cole.

Each night we set up camp with rocks around its edges, preventing howling winds from penetrating our tent. We decided to both sleep in the same tent to maximize our chances of staying warm. Meals are made on a portable gas stove in the entrance of the tent which consists of mainly canned stews and pastas, which are often if not always half cooked. Steve rightly mentions: "This will possibly be diarrhea." In between meals we nibble on a piece of beef jerky and some bone-dry bread, not providing nearly enough energy that our bodies yearn for.

On one of these nights I leave my sleeping bag for a special assignment. Years earlier I wrote in a poem that I would bury the engagement ring of my ex fiancé on the world's highest mountain. Since the time she had sent hers back in an envelope I was carrying both rings on a string around my neck. Being a man of my word, I dig a hole in the frozen ground until dirt heaps under my fingernails. I keep on digging until I can't feel my hands anymore, which is only about a foot deep. Wailing stars bear witness as I abandon the gold, never to see the light of day again. Trifling ice crystals form in my lashes in this personal ritual to close off with things from the past, in order to no longer hinder me. Surely one of the many advantages of traveling is having plenty of time to complete certain processes that otherwise would have been left undealt with.

Advancing our cause, we quickly run out of food. Furthermore, our altimeter was sent into the afterlife, unfortunately never again able to tell us our altitude. The risk increases exponentially when oxygen levels drop, that is when it's time to go back. Living to see another day holds more value than gambling your life for the purpose of pride. A returning climber invites us to join him to West Base Camp for a cup of hot chocolate. Arriving at the scene it becomes much more than that. We are being stuffed with tuna, cheese, hefty meals of macaroni and pretty much all we can eat. Sitting in a large circle we introduce ourselves and share stories with the overly generous group. They will not be easily forgotten, the amicable climbers of the British Army Expedition of 2006.

After placing the bi-colored flag of my hometown on an *inuksuk* (piled rocks placed by different individuals) of which a picture actually makes it into a Dutch newspaper after writing to the mayor, we move along.

As of yet I was completely unaware that three months from now, standing close to the highest place on earth, in the cold, I will coincidentally be at the lowest place on earth, in the heat, surrounded by salt, ash and sulfuric fumes, being at the Dead Sea at approximately four hundred fifteen meters below sea level.

Acuminate rocks with snow are our trail. Equipment is starting to get heavy on the shoulders. At one point, we have to cross a savage river. Water gushes down through pure ice on eroded rocks and our only possible option of reaching the other side is by a naturally formed ice bridge. It is basically a mini glacier. Even if it were to partially collapse, we would perish. Footprints of yaks makes the passage somewhat trustworthy. Many hours in search of more oxygen passes until we are close to where we began. On the path we catch up with a man with a big professional camera. Bingo, this has to be one of the crew members hired by the enterprising Australian boy. While inquiring about his experiences he brings fantastic news: "Lincoln, the writer, lives!" Since we heard him die over the walkie-talkie we do not believe it at first and assure him that he must be mistaken. After turning on his camera, he shows footage of this very morning, Lincoln carried by Sherpas and later sitting on the back of a yak, alive! Here's how it happened: over twelve hours after last radio contact surprising news enters Base Camp. Another team, just ascending, finds him sitting on a rim suffering from hypothermia, altitude sickness, cerebral edema and snow blindness. His coat open and half-uncovered he says: "I can imagine you are surprised to see me here." He had spent a whole night without oxygen, without a tent nor any proper protection. Surviving this is truly a miracle. Immediately this expedition team takes action and instructs the coordinators from Base Camp who on their turn alert a team of Sherpas to rescue him. What a story!

The three of us share merry moments as we hike back to Everest Base Camp. Well what do you know? Once there, we are invited to have dinner at the big orange tent of Seven Summits. When food is served Dutch climber Harry Kikstra himself sits next to me, but we exchange but a few words. He just lost his client on the mountain. The German Mister Weber lies forever in the treacherous white abyss. Understandably, a sacrifice that weighs heavy on the man's shoulders. Having lost someone for the second year in a row, he realizes his career as a professional guide has taken a nasty turn, perhaps even jeopardizing the legitimacy of his company. Having said that, I would still blindly follow someone with so much experience, trusting him with my life. Grim faces turn themselves to bed leaving Steve and I alone at the table. Out of respect we agree not to sleep in their tent tonight.

It is already around midnight and we are too tired to set up our own tents. Recalling the presence of Tibetan yurts with a fireplace only half a mile away, we set out to spend the night there. Lights of the mini village enticingly call out our names. So close to comfort yet so far removed. First, large pebbles slow us down, later we are halted by a fierce river that was just a tiny peaceful stream a week ago. Melted ice from the unforgiving Himalaya is our enemy. Do not think the black of night intends to lend a hand. With rolled-up pants we enter the ice-cold river that rapidly reaches our hips. Supporting each other by the arm, strong currents try to gulp us to the underworlds. Head torches guide us thirty feet across to the other side. While we are shaking from the cold we seek shelter in one of the yurts. The owners, an old married couple of which the woman is doing all the work, are surprised to find us at this hour and in this moist condition. Here we can allow our soaked clothes to dry, and the consolation of warm blankets put an end to this crazy adventure, and hopefully, to my pounding headache.

Before resuming the journey on the motorbikes I need to visit the bathroom. The nearby concrete shithole facility lacks toilet paper, which means a creative solution has to be found. It is a bit raw on the sphincter, yet the chance of a lifetime. Currency is worth almost nothing you know. Today I reckon myself a millionaire with adequate shame, holding contempt for the poor. How many people can say that they have wiped their ass with money? It is far from recommendable but it certainly does the trick.

During the day, sand wave roads bring us to dead end town Tingri. It is here that we fill our tummies with greasy pork, the only thing on the menu. Our dirty plates are full of fat and bones and it appears that no one knows where the actual meat goes. Our beat-up tires continue to spin further south as we get to see mesmerizing Lhotse, the third tallest mountain, and of course the connecting Mount Everest from another angle, towering above all its surroundings.

As the day progresses we are driving on an endless straight dirt track, brownish in complexion. Unsuspectingly a prodigious event occurs. It starts with white dots appearing on the horizon. Slowly but steadily it becomes clear that the highest peaks reveal themselves one more time in full glory. Engines stop to dwell in the moment while ancient winds breathe life into our nostrils. On the opposite side of the valley the entire Himalaya range is revealed one more time, the clear day introducing resplendent chromatism differentiating from the virgin snow. In all its might it is unexpectedly also a spiritual experience. Who knows if there is much more to the sages that were written thousands of years ago. Not necessarily agreeing with them but I sense a deep understanding on why this far-away culture worships the mountains of sovereign allure. They can discern the love and greatness of the divine Creator in their own way. Regardless of religion or my own set of beliefs one thing is certain: standing here on the desolate plateau, you just know that there is more between heaven and earth. Perhaps, yes perhaps, because here those two lie closest to each other.

5

NEPAL

These days different shades of grey grace the palette of the outstretched heaven. Brave rays of light pierce the natural blanket of condensation, fighting to save the zeal. Majestic Tibet, once honored by being a country of its own, now a province of communistic China, is about to wave farewell. Make no mistake, although it feels like leaving a trusted friend behind, the magic is not planning to end. In fact not at all.

It is always a challenge to find a place to crash when you are so tired you can barely stand. Except for now my mate Steve and I end up staying at the moldy diner where we just finished our evening meal, ensuring a roof above our heads. Brown tiles of the freezing floor force us to grab our sleeping bags and try out the timber benches, usually reserved for customers. A thermos with the highly addictive beverage of chai tea is the only comfort in another sleepless and rainy night. We had promised the owner to push the motorcycles out before he opens. In doing so giving him enough time to set everything back in order. Not to mention getting rid of the fumes of gasoline. Being true to our word the day starts very early, yet another day of breathtaking beauty has her waylay.

Descending the world's highest plateau the most amazing thing happens. A tree appears! I never knew you could appreciate a tree so much. Soon more follow until we really leave the bleakness behind. For at least a month we were trapped in rocks and ice, expelled from warmth and colors, far removed from liveliness. The further down we go the more the temperature rises. Bird sounds have never been so vivid and expressive, it does not take long before everything turns green and even into lush jungles with waterfalls and wildlife. It is truly indescribable to witness the birth of life again as in the first days of creation itself when the first stems sprung up. Finally, we can remove some of the layers from the outfits we are wearing. Moving along the following scene certainly stirs the cultural senses. If it wasn't for the tropical climate to spill the beans the border is near, for sure the sudden tin string of unending traffic now is. Driving on a dirt road, we pass ridiculously embellished trucks as well as American school busses, hardly recognizable due to the multitude of decorations and surplus of bright colors. Local men are wearing funny hats; local women are wearing beautiful dresses and have adorned themselves with jewelry and hemp tattoos on their hands. Slaloming nimbly between vehicles we reach border control.

Our good mood changes swiftly when we are bound to wait for four damn hours. Of course, Customs smell money thinking we are illegally exporting the motorcycles. Which in fact we are doing, but they do not need to know that! We tell them that we will return to China within a month and to avoid a scene we sign some dodgy documents to confirm that. Moreover, they find it rather peculiar that we cannot show them an entrance permit to Tibet, it was a streak of luck that Customs were not bothered by that too much. Literally on the other side of the fence there is a time difference of two hours. *Who has that?* Going through no-man's land, a hazardous muddy race track, littered with fist-size rocks, leads to our prize. Full of excitement we show up at the border of the Kingdom of Nepal!

Changing the currency from renminbi to rupees is not a problem but actually getting into the country proves to be difficult. Customs are not amused with the absence of license plates on our bikes. By Customs I mean blue-camouflaged soldiers, roughnecks armed up to the bone. Machine guns, barbed wire, concrete bunkers with watchtowers and sandbags. What is going on here?

To make things worse, in the office an angry-faced man is pointing at my tattoos. Turns out having a sleeve in this culture pretty much equals a few years jail time. Judging from this alone they reckon me as some sort of a hard case. The rotating fan on the ceiling somewhat cools my nerves. A sweaty man in a white shirt, too tight for his posture, also smells money on us thinking that we are planning to illegally import our bikes. Just to add, that is exactly our plan, but again he doesn't need to know that! He is willing to declare our entry on one condition alone: to be gone in fourteen days. By now, it is almost a habit to avoid their ridiculous demands, so we lie that we will leave the country in no time. Again, we sign some dodgy documents. At this particular moment in my life, I am so naive I do not even care to watch my back in the next couple of months I spend in Nepal. I guess boys will be boys.

Crossing foxholes and roadblocks, we leave the border behind and penetrate deeper into lands that I know nothing about. A week prior to today I didn't even know that I would be here right now. That sure spices things up a bit! The oncoming traffic immediately intimidates us by dangerously driving on our side of the road. People yell and scream, almost deliberately wanting to start a fight. Some ghost-riding guys on a moped also try to hit us. This is getting crazy! By the time a huge truck almost flattens us in a curve the penny finally drops. Shit it's *us* driving on the wrong lane! What do you know? This is how we find out over here they drive on the left side of the road.

Serpentine trails continue the rest of the day through green hills. Large fields of cornstarch are everywhere as well as basic straw huts for people to live in. Grey cows, looking very different from the ones I am used to, appear skinny. A clear blue sky and intense sun certainly lift our spirits. Even the armed soldiers seem to be getting friendlier at the passing of each frequent check post. Very slippery mud roads with deep truck tracks are a pain in the ass though. At one point the vibrations of the road actually become too much for my Jialing to handle. Suddenly my backpack is dragging along through the mud. Chinese iron is just too weak; my entire luggage rack on the back has broken off. Seriously? Although it sucks, at this point it is not even surprising anymore when something breaks. With certain effort some cable-tides do the trick. At least as long as it lasts.

When evening falls we are treated on a visual spectacle as hundreds, if not thousands, of joyful fireflies fizzle about. Nighttime grants asphalt again, and with it a chaotic number of lorries without particle filters, cars, motorcycles, tuk-tuks, and weird motorized vehicles, collectively responsible for an insane pollution. Our lungs are in hot pursuit of oxygen and our faces are left blackened from fumes and dust. When my scarf is fully congested I feel the sand grinding between my teeth. The purest of nature from before has now given way to a suffocating urban complex. Until finally, later than expected the capital Kathmandu shakes our hand with its sweaty groin. Without navigation, a road map or knowing the way in the first place, it is crazy to know that we drove precisely where we wanted to go. It must be written in the stars or something. In a city completely new to us we arrive in the touristy part, characterized by canopies on the facades, the dirty abandoned streets of Thamel.

Exhausted from the trip, my Canadian travel buddy and I desire to spend a week in the hotel we checked in to. Unfortunately, after only one night we are on the move again. While Steve is enjoying the luxury of a warm shower it goes completely unnoticed that the drain is clogged. Things are already floating in the room by the time I wake up. A few floors down water is dripping from the ceilings. By the time I yell: "Turn it off!", the owner is already knocking on the door. As I open the brown door a small tsunami heads for the hallway, the miniature billows reaching up to his ankles, soaking his shoes. We quickly grab our belongings, wish him all the best, and get the hell out of there.

Another hotel seems slightly better. All is fine and dandy except for an out-of-order toilet. Just when everything seems to be going well the staff steals half the amount of gasoline from our jerry can. Needless to say, we leave without paying for our stay.

The next hotel with a private bathroom is so inexpensive that I am not even considering a hostel with a dormitory, let alone enduring a shared kitchen. Restaurants are cheap enough for daily visits, which is a good thing as I love food. To outsmart the insects I try my luck a few times tying my fresh bread from the bakery to the ceiling lamp. Yet a horde of malicious ants finds it every time, careless about their incursion.

One of these afternoons I climb the two hundred thirteen steps of *Dharahara*, better known as the Bhimsen Tower. Marveling the view of the entire valley I am yet oblivious of the future earthquake that would bury almost two hundred people in the rubble of this structure alone, and a staggering total death toll of nearly nine thousand! Not ending there, nearly twenty-two thousand become wounded, leaving thousands upon thousands homeless and displaced. I suppose it was always a matter of when, instead of if, the earthquake would happen, after being warned for years in advance because Kathmandu is built on a rather large fault line.

Luckily spared from such misfortune this district has plenty of tumult to get engaged in. The streets are infused with protests, strikes and political rallies. Carrying banners and placards, they march through the streets, shouting and chanting, by the hundreds and even by the thousands at times. Gathering on squares and fields it goes on for weeks. It's a privilege to experience Nepal still as a monarchy. You see, a coup and overthrow of the standing government by the rebels who are hungry for power and vehemently idealistic was inevitable. As threatening as the heavily armed military was upon entry, we are accustomed to it by now. Feeling great about our new habitat, meaning the country, we reckon it's time to indulge ourselves in some laid-back adventure and well-deserved leisure.

Something that starts as a mere thought develops into a memory for life. Funny how that works. Amazing what can happen in a few days. It all starts with a long sticky bus ride to the southwest. It is very relaxing to not have to drive ourselves for a change. Photo cameras are snapping away at all the green beauty about. Fairly dark-skinned people are working in the fields, tilling and plowing the ground with outdated tools. Their bodies a bit beyond slim – skinny perhaps. Children yet unaware of the poor conditions seem shy but happy, also they are looking very adorable in those mandatory school uniforms. For different reasons I highly support the use of such uniforms, I think all schools around the world should implement this, as kids should feel equal and safe to be themselves. Later we trade the bus for an outdated van with its sliding door missing. Sitting in the opening, I let the warm wind go through my hair as I observe everyday life. I enjoy this moment to the full; in my own country, burdened by too many rules and restrictions, this would never be allowed. Time moves along until we reach a broad brown river with a slow current. Small crocodiles are minding their own business at the muddy shore. Locals in primitive canoes paddle us across where we are embraced by the loving arms of the Royal Chitwan National Park.

A white jeep with an open back takes us on a wobbly ride to a huge track of lush boscage, as yet unspoiled by mass tourism. In fact, upon arrival we discover that we are the only ones! Subtropical heat and the sun gently caress our faces. Some of the staff from the park are so bored that they serve fresh juices every fifteen minutes, others stuff us with delicious local dishes all day. Could life be more perfect? Yes it can, because today we hop on an elephant for the first time for a ride through the jungle. Boy, is that fun! In awe of these powerful intelligent creatures, we are inseparable from them from first contact on. So how does it work? Have you ever seen someone mount the largest land animal? It goes as follows: place your foot on the front side of the lowered trunk, gently grab the elephant's ears which magically makes the trunk go upward, then step onto its head and walk to the middle of its back and *voilà*, you now find yourself on top of it, and on top of things. I understand when people are against the use of animals for commercial profit, but this is not like those half-gnawed circus bears with chains around their necks in Bulgaria in the 1950s or something. From what we see, the elephants are very well treated. Park rangers play with them all day, clean them, massage them, feed them – and both parties seem to enjoy it. There are always folks claiming that elephants are wild animals; however, I see no reason why man and animal cannot coexist. I mean, why should we live apart in nature?

On one of our jungle endeavors, our grey friend even protects us. We spot a group of rhinos between the five-foot-high grass in the swamplands. It is less than ten minutes before one of them, the biggest one, is fed up with our presence. Just when the snarling savage is closing in to announce his attack, something completely unexpected happens: without any warning, our trunked ride goes full beast mode, no pun intended. It starts chasing the rhino, crushing anything in its path! Sitting on the elephant's back, we have to actively protect ourselves from the branches coming our way. With brutal force thin trees are stomped down and we trail blaze through an increasingly dense forest, pursuing the rhino until he is out of sight. What a thrill! In addition, it certainly looks like our taxi was protecting us instead of itself, which makes sense if you see the bond between the elephants and people. Especially with their caretakers – but in this case, us also. The adults even have enough trust to let us feed the babies and arm-wrestle with their little trunks, which are already shockingly strong. Being so close to beings that could kill you in an instant is a humbling experience. Spending time in an area as untouched as this, I truly fathom how important it is for humans to interact and build relationships with animals.

Although the park is close enough to the border with northeast India for us to smell the curries, our time in Nepal has not yet ended. Another crowded and worn-out bus takes us to a blooming paradise at the foot of the extensive Himalayan range. Halting near a big lake we arrive in foliate Pokhara. The city lies in the shadow of Fishtail, a snow-capped mountain left untouched due to its sanctity. At present, fortune seekers overrun the city, kind of ruining the atmosphere by turning all the buildings into restaurants – very much unlike the olden days, when swarms of climbers flocked to climb the breathtaking Annapurna.

Experienced mountaineers as well as juvenile daredevils and nature freaks – everyone is getting along. A feel-good town, characterized by invisible geckos sticking to your ceiling and cockroaches boldly engaging in a Cooper test on your bed sheets – you gotta love it. Nevertheless, I feel an inner peace that I have not felt in a long time. Lying on the roof of a cheap hotel with the enchanting outlook of a perfect sunset across the ancient lake is phenomenal. The orange roof tiles remain warm from the prosperous day. As if that wasn't enough, my Discman is playing Coldplay's greatest hits. This might come across as awkward, but sometimes you have to give yourself a few days off while traveling.

For Steve it is nearly time to go home. His airplane leaves in a few days. For that reason, we plan to take the bus back to Kathmandu. Within an hour of bidding the serenity farewell, we are stuck in traffic. The cracked road with two lanes is jam-packed. While the hands of our watches are spinning round we don't move an inch. Due to the boiling hot temperature, I decide to check the surroundings, and while doing so I walk nearly half a mile until I discover what the fuss is all about. There is a dead guy in the street! A large group of bystanders are following the debate between hysterical family members of the deceased individual and the bus driver who is apparently responsible for killing the man; the driver is now trying to make a financial agreement. Turns out Nepal does not have insurance policies yet. A random German tourist and I reckon that the hold-up has lasted long enough. Therefore, we step in, intending to drag the lifeless body to the side of the street. There are only about a million cars waiting to resume their agenda, and to us it is logical and productive thinking. Just when we bend over to grab the wrists and ankles, a few police officers jump on our backs, ready to club us down! Several attempts to persuade them to continue their quarrel *next* to the road and not *on* it ultimately fail. It is here and now that we learn that everyone is subject to Nepal's nonsensical laws. On the other hand, it might be pretty darn disrespectful of us to deviate so far from their customs, but the thinking of our young European minds is inscrutable.

Back in the center of the anarchic capital we saunter through dusty Thamel, spending our last moments together. A newspaper at a wooden kiosk surprises me when I read the story of Lincoln – you know, the writer on Sagarmatha, as the Nepalese call Mount Everest. To our disappointment, it only mentions the expeditionary team that found him, instead of the true heroes, the brave Sherpas who also went up and actually got him down alive. That is a slice of the reporting skills of the mainstream media for you. Even more jaw-dropping is the second paragraph, which reveals that in China workers managed to cram in the last seventy kilometers of the train track between Beijing and Lhasa into just a few weeks. Unbelievable! Reading those things that I more or less personally been involved in, my heartbeat goes up a notch from the excitement.

With much joy, we look back on our chapter together. It was a time of deep and meaningful conversation, where we shared memories such as the time when a pink-dressed female marching band started to play because we walked by, and when we had to go to the hospital for

Steve's peanut allergy. Sitting there with his swollen face the nurse sterilized a needle by holding it above a lit candle. We would never forget the time when we had a meeting in a dicey hotel with the Nepalese Mafia, who wanted to discuss the smuggling of diamonds across the border. Realizing that these fellows were not your everyday kind of pickpockets, we cunningly played along, trying to keep things friendly, and trying to bail out of the deal by purposely setting our going rate too high. Still, when the sunglasses-wearing bodyguards of the head figure – who was radiating serious authority like the character in the gangster movie *The Godfather* – locked the door behind us, the first thing I instinctively checked was whether there was plastic sheeting on the floor. And then there was the time when the hairy Canadian fell because his legs were just a little bit too short for his bike, and all the times we had to mentally pull each other through due to the insane hardships. If I may say so myself, this has been a pretty remarkable journey for two strangers.

Left by myself again in this big world, I get on the *hoser*'s donated bike to drive from the district of Pulchowk to Patan, where I drop it off with one of his vague contacts. In fact, it is at one of the branches of the United Nations where it's probably still present at today. On my own motorcycle again, I am joined by Ram Kumar, the teenage bellboy from my hotel. After driving through unimaginable pollution and sheer pandemonium, we arrive at Pashupatinath, where one is taken back in time by centuries, if not millennia. At this remarkable site, human bodies burn twenty-four hours a day. Hindus do not believe in burying their dead – instead, they are cremated on the same day they die, pretty much out in the open, covered by some twigs. As a non-Hindu you must watch the rituals from across the Bagmati River, but my new friend arranges to get me in, despite it being a very rare opportunity for a Westerner. Next to the burning corpses, on small-bricked platforms, family members of the deceased are shaving their heads in the traditional way while surrounded by white smoke. High temples with Pagoda architecture shine in a dignified manner on both sides of the river, where the ashes and human remains are swept into, only to meet women doing their laundry just a couple of hundred yards downstream. A reminder of a once-so-advanced civilization, double-layered copper rooftops adorned with real gold gleam over all the surroundings. According to legend, the temple is one of the oldest in Nepal. It makes you wonder where it all went wrong?

While walking up to nearby Arya Ghat, I realize that the path is crawling with disease-infested monkeys. They are everywhere, and keeping an eye on anything they can snatch. Although I am only six feet tall, I pass locals who are at least a head shorter, making me feel like a giant.

The bellboy proposes to visit his uncle and aunt that are living close by. My hesitation vanishes as snow in sunshine when he mentions that he has two beautiful nieces. The Don Juan that I am, I was very much interested to meet them. Although it turns out the girls are not at home, we spend many hours talking. In a way, it is an honor to be the first white guest. *Uncle* is wearing thick spectacles and a black mustache with some grey at the ends. He is delighted to show me the albums with family portraits, even more so, his homegrown vegetables on the rooftop which he takes much pride in. These kindhearted and entertaining folks show great hospitality.

Back in Thamel I'm introduced to the 'fucking-girl', whom we meet in the unpaved streets. She greets me with a certain amount of shame in her big blue eyes, at the same time somehow aware of my commiseration. So the rumors I heard are true. Here is this seventeen-year-old French girl boldly prostituting herself to supposedly buy a ticket back home. With her curly hair and doll-like face, she pretty much visits every single room of the entire hotel, except for mine. God knows how she ended up in this situation, but I guess we all have our crosses to bear. In an era before the invention of WhatsApp, and before Facebook was in our daily vocabulary, now a decade later, on a relaxing Sunday morning during breakfast, I can still dwell on whatever became of her.

A series of small events make the weeks go by fast. For one, with a mic and camera I was interviewed by journalists about the wrongly adjusted mile gauges in taxis. Recently a client was pummeled down with an iron rod by a driver over this, thus sparking the controversy. Several times indeed, misleading cab drivers almost had me pay quadruple the actual price had I not paid close attention. You bet I pissed off some drivers by keeping an eye on it.

On the day I apply for my visa to India, three fakirs have placed some wicker baskets on a rug, more or less in the middle of the street. Producing annoying melodies on their flutes, I am invited to sit amongst them on the rug. Unable to control my curiosity I accept. If I had only known what would happen next. When the lids go off the baskets, the first snakes are pulled out and carelessly placed on my shoulders. In no time I have a total of six snakes around my neck and the seventh, a cobra, is staring me right in the face. I can only pray the fakirs know what they are doing. I did not sign up for this! By no mean is it the fakir's intention to see me die on the spot, because in a hypnotizing manner he starts whispering into my ear claiming that I'll give them a lot of money. I respond that I will give them whatever they want as long as they get that cobra out of sight – needless to say, I lied.

Then there is the homeless boy in the streets, six, maybe seven? They are always small for their age anyway, it is hard to tell. I buy him two pieces of bread, which he later sells back to the baker at the side door and goes off to buy crack. My heart breaks as I tail the kid out of interest and compassion. I walk back to the bakery, look the man straight in his eyes while helping myself to fill my daypack with bread, with the most contemptuous glim. His employees wonder why their boss does not say anything about me stealing the bread, but he recognizes me instantly and shame is dripping off his face.

Incidents like this make it very hard to trust the people around here. Stepping out of that constant prejudiced state of mind, I take a huge leap of faith when one guy asks for a stack of medicine. I honestly admit, I do not trust him at all, thinking he will sell it back to the pharmacy. He claims he is going to die without medicine and judging from the way he looks he certainly has a point. His appearance is like a person from the 1990s with severe HIV on a hunger strike. Clever as I am, I take the strips of pills and prescriptions out of the boxes so he cannot resell them, and make a list of his obligations. After vanishing from the street scene for six weeks I convince myself that I have been scammed after all. The bastard! But lo and behold, when I run into him again his festering wounds have healed and he gained a dozen pounds! I am very content to see him so healthy and fresh. Years later it sinks in that I might have actually saved the young man's life. Amazing how those dark sunken eyes transformed into this beautiful bright smile. Still remembering his face as if it was yesterday, I become emotional just thinking about it. Miracles do exist.

If not hindered by frequent power cuts, I delve into my email to see my friends probing me as to what I do all day. Yet how does one explain that there is no time to get bored? Such a great mix! Armed with bullhorns and banners, protests and political rallies continue almost on a daily basis. Streets are filled with stands and stores that offer colorful tapestries, gems, jewelry, native handicrafts and loads of shiny glittering objects. Tourists from all over the world stop here to enjoy the unity of travelers, the surplus of yoga lessons, smoked corn on the cob for a nickel and dime in the squares, with vegan style restaurants abound, ancient stupas to be marvelled at and always a possibility to help out in a school or one of the many orphanages. Meanwhile rickshaws almost knock you down with the smell of incense from the many roadside shrines. What do you mean: "What do you do all day?"

While roaming the neighborhood I am asked to buy a handmade pouch by some teenage girls. I reply that I do not need one of those, but after thinking out loud perhaps I can assist in generating some income by helping out their cause to sell their merchandise to tourists. Instead of money, only strange looks are received from unsuspecting passers-by. A new friendship is born. From that moment on we are hanging out every chance we get. The oldest of fifteen is also the fattest and clearly the leader of the group. She has the biggest mouth but perhaps also the biggest heart. Rita functions as a mother for her younger sister Sangita, a friend with a similar name, also known as Sunita, and the others Parbati and Maya. Later that same week we visit the cinema together for the latest Bollywood movie 'Krrish', and during lunch the girls luxuriate over pizza, as for the last fifteen years or so they have been eating *dal bhat* with *masala* every single day, which is one of the traditional dishes consisting of boiled rice and spices.

On one of the Saturdays we walk two hours straight to check out a church in another part of town. "It's walkable," they said. Dawdling their cheap flip-flops along irregularities of dirty roads with their tongue hanging out from their mouths, it demonstrates quite a challenge. As a way of not offending anyone, they left the red dot between their eyes at home. We leave our footwear in the hall and walk in barefoot. It's not a problem that we are a little late; the service lasts five freaking hours! Sitting on the concrete floor with a boney ass and not understanding a word of the sermon, I praise the heavens when it is over. All this waiting is not in vain however, as I am approached by a beautiful girl from the United States who is volunteering for an evangelical organization. Wavy dark hair, together with those dark eyebrows with light oculars beneath them, and a voice likened to a merry lullaby, a slim body and a playful nose ring. I had been checking her out during the service and she is intrigued at how I ended up here with five teenagers she happens to know. As we decide to catch up later in the day, I think to myself that I never reckoned a church to be the place to pick up chicks.

Without use of words it becomes apparent that the all-American girl and I are very fond of each other. Every time we meet we talk for hours and hours, until we get kicked out as the last ones at restaurants at three in the morning. Where the staff is already sleeping on chairs slotted together, or until the first women go out to the well to fill their pitchers, which is usually around five. We walk and we talk through all of nature's hurdles, whether it be thirty degree Celsius heat (the cause of my sunburned legs) or being showered down from the first signs of the Monsoon – we are simply inseparable. Thus, on a given afternoon, we end up climbing the many stairs of Swayambhunath, a five-hundred-year-old Buddhist temple on top of a hill. Clearly visible from several places from the valley down below. Unhindered by time it stands out on account of a white stupa with a gold helicoid. Black-painted eyes of the omniscient god are intoxicating to say the least. The religious shrine is better known as the Monkey Temple, obviously because it is packed with monkeys. One of those scallywags set his sights on the pineapple on a stick we are enjoying and launches an attack. From off a ledge to the ground he jumps up in a split second and reaches for the stick, biting the girl in her calf, his fierce canines sinking into human flesh. What happens next is something I will never forget. I'm not making this up. She screams from the pain while at the same time cursing the animal in the name of Jesus! I do not know if I should laugh or be amazed. When I chase the monkey away and check her leg, I am dumbfounded to see it without a single scratch. Call it more than meets the eye but maybe the black-painted eyes of Buddha had seen it all happen.

When the time approaches to leave this beautiful country I spend every day with the teenage pouch-selling girls from the street. Parbati, the most beautiful one, invites me to her home. She lives with her

97

mother and grandfather in a dirty wooden shack. They actually own a cow that provides for most of the income. Meeting the family, I quickly realize that I am baited into an awkward situation. Her mother more or less proposes for us to get married, as a way of securing her old days with this supposed walking white treasure chest. In Nepali culture the age gap is not much of an issue, so that is tackled, and she is definitely appealing. Raised with a Western mindset I simply cannot marry a child. Having said that, I am not the boogieman either and make her mother happy after all. Converted to an X amount of dollars, equal to a mere couple of hours of work in my own country, she can enjoy schooling for a year and her sister will receive a new stack of schoolbooks.

In the grubby streets the girls try to teach me their language and show me around. After getting to know each other a little more, I really begin to care for them. That they also begin to care for me I find out when I become really ill. For days I am plagued by heavy vomiting and experience the pleasure of squirting hot gravy out of my behind, the acid burning away the enamel of the toilet. Presumably I ate something very bad. Incapable of leaving my hotel room they show up at the door to bring a net of oranges and water, bless their hearts. Because I need to run to the bathroom every five minutes, I try to send them away. Moving heaven and earth they refuse to heed my requests and do not give up easily. Insisting for thirty minutes, I'm finally swayed to let them in. Who knows maybe they will provide some distraction from the discomfort. And that is exactly what they do as one of them accidentally types the wrong access code on my cellphone three times, immediately blocking it. The PUK code to reactivate the phone is stored in a taped-up cardboard box in an attic somewhere in the Netherlands. How convenient. Seeing how guilty the girl feels I try to laugh it off. What more can you do?

Dorje and Bindu, the owners of an internet cafe on the corner of the street where I have lunch pretty much every day, noticed that I have not been around lately. Concerned about my well-being they check with the manager of the hotel and learn about my situation. Without speaking to me first they hurry to the pharmacy and bring me all the medicine and groceries I need. How lovely is that couple. Thanks to them, I restore quickly after that.

Bear in mind the whole thing lasts for two weeks, leaving me malnourished and weak. For that reason, I am too tired to bring one of the girls home at night, as I often do, on the back of my motorcycle. She lives in another district only twenty minutes from where we are. It is way too dangerous to let her go alone at this ludicrous hour. I feel responsible for the situation and come up with a risky solution. Since Steve had left, I have an extra bed in my hotel room, so I decide to sneak her in. We climb over the fence and discreetly avoid the reception desk, rush up the stairs and quickly get into the room. If we are caught the people will probably hang me on the highest tree for this, but for now it seems the logical thing to do. Sunita is the youngest of the group and coming from the poorest family. She is only thirteen. Although the shower is less than lukewarm, she has not bathed in two weeks. Therefore, she does not complain at all. When she exits the bathroom with wet hair and a towel wrapped around her frail underfed body I realize she has not smelled so fresh before. She crawls up beneath the blankets with a smile of satisfaction, showing her intense white teeth. As I switch off the work lamp, standing on an ugly brown nightstand dividing the two beds, she tells me this is the first time in her life that she will be sleeping on a mattress. Back home her family is so poor that she is used to sleeping on the floor. I think I am just in time turning around in my bed before the moonlight shining through the worn-out curtains reveals that I began to shed some tears. That just breaks my heart. Even if it was for this night alone, I am thankful her young bones experience the comfort of an actual bed, and she can truly rest.

Before the staff wakes up in the early hours I sneak her out of the complex to send her on her way to school. There we cannot be seen together also, so I have to let her go alone. At least the first daylight makes it free from direct danger. Now that I cannot protect her anymore, I keep watching her walk away until I lose her out of sight. Independent as they are I know the girls feel safe with me. Their own fathers are alcoholics and slackers.

That certainly explains why saying goodbye was such a heavy task. On the last day before I continue my trip, all the teenagers gather around to bestow a genuine present to me. I am speechless when it becomes clear that they saved all their earnings for this refined kashmir cloth. I shriek inside to not accept it and give it back, but on account of their culture that would be very disrespectful to them. With certain agony, I receive it. Of course, I am also very proud of them. The owner of the internet cafe puts a silk scarf around my neck and according to tradition wishes me *Tashi Delek*. I had no idea I was loved so much by the people, but when the whole neighborhood congregates to wish me farewell, I am deeply touched. So much so that I don't hesitate to put on my goggles, in case they notice my wet eyes. It really feels like leaving home. Sound of the engine echoes through the familiar narrow streets. As I might never return, I allow one last peek into my mirror while raising my hand, before vanishing in the cloud of pollution from the traffic. Far removed from being good to go, but there I go, completely alone again, embarking on a journey filled with prodigy.

Kathmandu, believe it or not, is the only city in a different time zone as opposed to the rest of the world. That in itself already makes this place supernatural. Driving through the city's traffic all the way past the outskirts, is absolute mayhem. Coming out from the valley it is nothing less of a relief when red-bricked communities make way for overgrown hills and lavish green mountains. Winding roads are overshadowed with huge overhanging plants due to the escarpment, the splendor of bright flowers as well as this typical humid smell in the air. Advancing this trip without company makes me feel lonely, I need to get used to not having the privilege anymore of directly sharing my experiences with another human being. Providentially, the awe-inspiring view across the extended sequence of valleys with a clear sky gives me some comfort. The route leads two hundred kilometers west until I unintentionally end up in the unwinding hotspot of Pokhara again. Having an impulsive moment, I intercede with the original plan to crash here for a few days. Just having escaped the snarl I convince myself a mini-vacation is deserved.

Everything is still here: friendly people, the majestic bay with colorful fishing boats, and the viewpoint from Sarangkot where sunlight on the eternal snow produces millions of flickering stars. The staff of the hotel I stayed at before are pleased to meet the notorious motorcycle that goes with the plethora of stories I had shared on my previous encounter.

Fish straight from the lake with fresh mango juice and French fries. Although I order the exact same meal every day at a cozy restaurant on the street corner, the owner, who is a huge woman as wide as she is tall, pulls back a chair and sits herself across the table to take my order. In spite of her heart of gold I feel sympathy for the plastic lawn chair that almost literally weighs down under immense pressure. As in the days prior to this one, she tries to hook me up with her daughter who has not yet reached the age of twenty. By all means, not meaning to boast but this happens almost everywhere I go. You get used to this brazen conduct after a while, but it's still flattering.

With a setting like this, it is effortless to be entertained. Everything is going fine until I'm told there will be a beach festival on one of these nights. When the time comes, the manager of the hotel insists that I should join the self-proclaimed party animal. In doing so, he is very persuasive. Having had my fair share of amusement when I was younger (in fact as a semi-professional dancer at clubs and raves from Miami to Ibiza, and occasionally performing for Calvin Klein International), I choose to keep on lounging on the sofa in the reception hall. With a head full of new impressions, it's nice to just relax and watch movies sometimes. There is probably no MDMA anyway, although nowadays drug use is extensively remote of my normal range of things that I enjoy. He goes on by deviously offering to buy me all my drinks, however, and this may surprise you, alcohol has never entered my esophagus. I just can't stand the taste of it. You cannot find smoking or drinking in my dictionary. By the time the manager realizes that he simply can't get me out of that sofa he suddenly pulls the trump card out of his sleeve. "My four friends will be coming along," he says while showing unframed pictures of gorgeous looking girls. Manipulated idiot that I am, I jump up and get ready for the night. A quick shower, a spray of deodorant and a dollop of hair gel makes me all groomed up. What's the worst that could happen?

Arriving back in the lobby the so-called friends just happen to walk in and without exaggeration they might be the prettiest girls in the whole freaking country. It was as if they walked out of some magazine. Once at the festival the manager is trying everything he can to render me drunk. It will not be long before I unravel his true intentions. Enjoying funky beats at the shoreline, we place ourselves in the soft grass, the four angels and I. Two of them do not shy away from kissing my neck and sticking their hands down my pants. This all happened way too easily, but even now I am dumb enough to not grasp what's going on. *This looks promising*, I actually think to myself, promptly raising the bar of my own simplicity. When they suggest going back to the hotel where they have a room, I know it's bingo. While the five of us are lying on the double bed the rude awakening finally kicks in. Entangled in this shameless scheme, the nothing but ordinary prostitutes want to see rupees first, aka cold hard cash. How could I have been so stupid to not have seen this one coming? This party is over. That scumbag of a manager probably gets his guests drunk all the time in order to do this despicable trick. He is a mother fucking P.I.M.P.! Disgruntled, I leave the room and walk up the stairways to go to my own bed. The problem is, I'm still horny as hell. Since there's only one option left I pathetically masturbate myself to sleep. Indeed, these are the difficulties one faces while traveling.

In retrospect, I am really happy nothing happened though. Being in the summer of 2006 I'm in the very middle of my self-commissioned seven years of celibacy, a promise that I almost broke, due to constantly having to fight the temptations. Friends and strangers alike call me crazy, and perhaps rightly so, yet to me this total abstinence of sexual relations is something I have to try in order to fulfil my spiritual journey. And what do you know? At the ending of this personal jubilee I actually complete my goal, making me feel more enlightened. Right after the seven years of pureness, it is inevitable for it not to backfire. I start sleeping with the girl next door who is in a relationship and I get addicted to filthy internet porn. That is right. I am embarrassed to be called a human being.

Lesson well learned. In any case, I will not let the incident tarnish my stay. In fact, I have something to look forward to. In a fortuitous turn of events, I meet Scott, a man from the United States, who also happens to know my pouch-selling friends from Kathmandu. With help from sponsors, he found means to treat the girls to a new set of fine robes, and a trip to Pokhara! How about that?

Through email contact, we know where to find each other. Upon their arrival, we catch each other from afar, as their jauntily yelling fills the street: "Dzjef! Dzjef!" It is funny to me how they have a hard time pronouncing my first name correctly.

When the generous American and one of his friends rent motorcycles for a day, they politely ask me to join. I answer I would like to but of course not without the girls. Without any form of hesitation, they agree. And so it happens. With the girls on the back and the sun in the sky we cruise alongside the lake. Being at the foot of the greenest foothills of the Himalayan range, it stretches far inland. Pale blue clouds smolder at the distant horizon. Everybody is having the time of their life. The air is filled with smells of freedom and independence. Encompassed by a blissful scenery of tranquility is the warm wind caressing the hairs on my arms while pacing the winding trail. Tiny birds frolic about. A feeling of peace of mind overtakes me. Except for teaching the kids how to swim, I do not remember the last time I really had to work. In this wandering existence where sometimes I don't even know where I am when I wake up, I feel at home, I feel alive, I feel loved. While having Parbati's arms around my waist, the channeling begins. Intense joy of these new friendships is healing to the soul. Even more so, they help erase wounds of a haunting past if you will, making space for new energy to indulge, thus revitalizing my whole well-being. *This*, is backpacking.

At nighttime after a neat candlelight dinner on the rooftop of a restaurant, we head to the lake, the two girls and I with whom I connected most with. Crashing on one of the bobbing fishing boats at the shore, deep conversations follow that move me beyond words. I learn that there was no real time for them to enjoy their childhood as they are hindered by the hard city life. Listening to their heartbreaking stories, I conclude they more or less skipped the adolescence phase and went straight into adulthood. I never thought that I could learn something from a couple of children, yet here we are. Where do you find such wisdom and soundness among the youth?

Saying goodbye on the last night in the mountaineer village is so much harder than a week ago. As if the kashmir cloth wasn't enough the girls now give something of personal value when we're congregated in their hotel room. Varying from something simple as a key chain to imitation jewelry, something that will help me remember them. Not that they have to worry about that. My memory collects the images of their richly flowing tears and with a fluttering lower lip I can hardly restrain myself. One by one, we hug goodbye until it is really time to go. Walking through the hallway of the hotel towards the exit they keep staring. Standing there with the doorknob in my hand, I turn around one last time, only to see them close together waving goodbye with wet cheeks and sad faces. With pain in my heart, I wave back and make it around the corner just in time, before I burst into sobbing. *God, I love these girls.* Maybe that is why, now thirteen years later, I still talk to them frequently on the phone. How amazing is it to witness them all growing up into beautiful women, getting married, and becoming responsible mothers themselves.

When I started the journey I had literally nothing planned beyond Tibet. So to be two days away from India is rather exciting. Gradually the skin tone of locals becomes darker. While moving west it is necessary to zigzag my way through the madness, avoiding cows, goats and chickens, huge potholes, and an occasional peacock. Wherever I have a small break to eat or pee I am exposed to villagers gathering around like a swarm of bees. If I could only describe what it's like to have zero privacy. It is especially inconvenient when stopping for number two for example. Nine out of ten times, it is impossible with all those eyes clinging to every move I make. A mere moment for myself is not allowed. Think about that for a second. They are so curious that I can't even take a shit. With reasonable pavement, I keep following my roadmap. Always accompanied by a close hot sun in the vast vaulted dome. What can go wrong?

Tell me this is not really happening. On a quiet country road, surrounded by banana trees, I am caught by my biggest fear. A flat rear tire! There I stand all alone in a remote area in a foreign country of which I do not speak the language. On top of that, I am not equipped to fix it myself because for some silly reason Steve and I split the tools on his departure. Black oxen in the surrounding muddy farmlands couldn't care less about my situation. Nobody among the sporadic passing traffic speaks English. However, by listening very carefully and paying close attention to hands, their non-verbal signs almost being a language of its own, I find out a mechanic is only six kilometers away. Unfortunately, in the direction I just came from. Trying to drive as slowly as possible fails instantly when the tube comes out and remains next to the rim, thus, leaving but one option left. A few years back during mountain biking through Belgium there was a heat wave, and I also got a flat rear tire. However, pushing that bicycle was a trillion times easier than now pushing my fully packed motorcycle under these conditions. Upon arrival at the open-air garage, my head is as red as a lobster, as well as my shoulders, with my clothes totally drenched in sweat. Meanwhile searching through my backpack for a fresh outfit there was a hollow consolation, as before I know it, the motorcycle is fixed.

With the minor incident putting me behind schedule I keep on driving until dusk. Not that I have an actual schedule, it is just that I felt like making some kilometers today. At one point, I notice a cozy spot to set up camp. A small open grass field right next to an entryway to the jungle seems fit. Having pulled over I throw up my beloved *The North Face* tent in an instant, securing myself for a successful overnight stay. Connecting bushes finally provide some privacy, without nosy eyes I return my disgusting never seen before lunch from this afternoon back to nature. Of course, it only takes a second for someone to show up. Right after the steamy pile of curry is literally and figuratively behind me, a young man approaches, and asks: "Are you sure you want to spend the night here?" I cannot think of a reason not to. Inquiring what the deal is it was better left unsaid. "This area is not uncommon for bears and tigers!" he replies, while excitedly nodding his head. Are you kidding me? To his credit, he does invite me to stay with his family, but I am too tired right now to pack my gear. After I give him some clothes as a gift, superfluous on account of the new temperatures, he is on his way again.

As you can imagine it is a little hard to catch any sleep. With a knife in hand, I turn to stone by the smallest sound of a cracking twig. It is a relief that I am at least alive at daybreak. Perhaps thanks to the huge dump I took yesterday the wildest animals are possibly kept at a safe distance. But if you think I am alone, think again. Around five in the morning, the first workers of the field stroll by and pause to observe, tight-lipped. Soon the whole nearby village comes out to watch me. Leaning on their spuds, they watch me in utter silence while I am cooking noodles for breakfast, packing up the tent and loading everything onto the motorcycle. I can't help but wonder what is going on in those silent minds of them. Having started the engine my mirrors show they begin to walk as I drive away. I fantasize that years from now, while walking to work they will poke each other saying: "Hey, do you remember the one time that this white lunatic pitched his tent here?"

Once I passed the medium-sized city of Mahendranagar things go fast. According to calculations, the border must soon follow. While moving along it's kind of hard not to notice that it becomes densely populated. I mean immensely densely populated. My goodness where do they all come from? Toward the west there are threatening watchtowers and heavily armed camouflaged foxholes on both sides of the road. Filled with roadblocks, barbed wire fences, army vehicles and trained soldiers, the scenery has all the characteristics of a war zone. Not to mention civilians with self-improvised carts dragging their bags and suitcases through the dirt, as well as animals, little children, and unimaginable junk that would be too much for a platoon of beachcombers. Military staff guide me to a creaky office where fat sweaty uniformed men ask questions and check my passport. Lucky for me there is zero exchange in information between border patrol and their other locations. They have no idea that I was only allowed to stay for two weeks! And just like that I have officially exited the country. Leaving behind a season of electrifying ampleness and with it undoubtedly a part of myself.

No less than six weeks of life-changing events in India follow of which you can read in the next chapter. After this, let's say, most challenging time, where dreams were crushed and my spirit tested, I make an unplanned visit to Kathmandu for a few weeks.

Arriving in the black of night I use public transport and my inner compass to find the hotel I was staying at before. Once located I catch the gate locked and all the lights are dimmed. With some effort I manage to lift my heavy backpack over the pointy gate, more like with a swing, then I go over it myself. The only thing breaking the silence now and then are barking stray dogs a few blocks away. Left to the courtly chestnut front door a barred window is slightly ajar. When I notice the silhouette of the bellboy sleeping on the floor I call out for him, so he can open the door to let me in. "Ram Kumar, Ram Kumar, it's me!" I strongly whisper. He wakes up to stare at me for a second and jumps out of bed. However, instead of going towards the door he stays in the corner of the room, not moving a muscle. I continue: "Hey man it's me, open the door!" When he becomes a living statue for ten minutes, I have literally no idea what is going on, then at one point he finally runs out of the room screaming, still not letting me in. Moments later stumbling sounds from the second-floor increase. I see lights turning on in several rooms now. Right upon seeing me, the owner of the hotel familiar with my face, quickly opens up, preventing me from having to spend a cold night out on the shady streets.

His loud uncontrollable laughter wakes up his staff members. Within minutes they gather about and everyone starts laughing riotously. Well what do you know? Turns out in the meantime, they had replaced the bellboy, the new one being terrified as hell from my sudden appearance! What a joke! He reckoned this white giant was there to take his life. The staff grab my luggage and carry it upstairs, checking in is unnecessary. Meanwhile the kid is still scared shitless and stands frozen behind the reception desk. Although I feel sorry for him we keep on cracking up. Quite the scene I cause within my first hour of being back in wondrous Nepal!

During the course of the succeeding weeks, I meet up with the all-American girl I met earlier on in church, with quite the postscript later on in life. Furthermore, many true wonders and fascinating miracles happen. In fact, they are so extraordinary that this book would fit into another category with an entirely different character had I written them here. Hence, I have decided those stories are for another place and for another time. *Namaste!*

6

INDIA

It is hard to separate the smells from the surplus of different dishes rising from roadside stalls, not to mention the penetrating odors of rotting muck. It's equally hard to believe your own eyes, concerning this untellable number of people roaming the area, which is in no way inferior to a very ill organized refugee camp. When I think about it, it might actually be one, and I'm in the middle of it. Thousands upon thousands creep about, like a human ant farm. You have to see it to believe it. Flies everywhere, skinny chickens running around and half-hairless dogs covered in sores look more dead than alive.

These are the very first impressions of the next country I am now acquainted with. Unfortunately, it pretty much lasts the whole duration of my stay. At the foot of this extremely inadequate piece of real-estate stands the immigration office, consisting of nothing more than sticks and large rags. Three bug-eyed civil servants with big bellies watch me approach in contempt. They do not speak a word of English and my Hindi is not what it used to be, but it is clear they are less than happy with my missing license plates on my motorcycle. After some verbal tug-of-war, I'm granted access into the bizarre lands of India.

The goal is to cross the concrete bridge over the wide part of the Mahakali river, the actual border, but how in the world can I? It is riddled with junk and animals, and I like to address once more without overstating the situation that the number of people is simply incomprehensible. Me being the only one with a motorized vehicle I have to find a way through the ocean of pedestrians, crammed in shoulder to shoulder. Due to sand, dust, and utter filth my scarf becomes hard to breathe through in no time. Effortlessly, everything gets sticky too. I am constantly paying close attention to make sure nobody steals anything from my luggage, the encompassing crowd however prevents even the slightest prospect of visibility. In no sooner than an hour I can finally shift to second gear and actually start driving, albeit slowly, but if you reckon me impervious from the next challenge you're mistaken.

For instance, traffic in Paris is quite bad, the traffic in South America is already worse, and traffic in an unorganized country like Egypt is definitely chaotic. However, the traffic here is downright suicidal. It is insanity at its best. Cars, trucks, scooters, from left to right and vice versa are so incredibly dangerous. No wonder this country has the most fatal traffic accidents every single year. It's like playing an incarnated video game of *Carmagaddon*. Cows, monkeys, massive potholes and people by the hundreds, if not thousands, are crossing the road without batting an eye. Even women with little children do not check incoming traffic; they just cross provincial roads and highways without first looking left or right, un-fucking-believable. I kid you not, even on the parts where I approach with 50mph, I have to kick locals aside, in doing so I almost fall myself. I repeatedly shout: "Get out of the way!" Moreover, I wave and pull the breaks in order to prevent impact. As if I do not exist, they keep ignoring me as well as other road users. Is this even real? Where am I? Then ladies and gentlemen, I present you the icing on the cake, there's the honking. Oh dear Lord the orchestra of eternal never ending honking, a multi-melodic blitzkrieg if you will. High pitch, low pitch, every pitch, the disorderly intonations aggressively resonate from every angle.

You know I never believed in evolution. I also reject even the slightest form of supremacy over another, and I certainly don't give a rat's ass about what race you descend from. But I swear on my two testicles that these creatures, at least the ones at this very location, are a different type of species. Because nobody can be *that* unintelligent, or in any case, so alarmingly irresponsible. It's almost like their brain capacity just doesn't match up. It leaves me without words and in a serious state of contemplation.

In a place where so many things can go wrong it was never a matter of *if* anything will happen, but *when*. And that moment is here. Driving on the left lane, as is custom in this country due to British colonization, I notice two impending lorries clearly driving too fast. For reasons unknown to a logical mind, the rear one decides to pass. The front one however, plagued with childish behavior, is not amused with this action and starts speeding up. Driving side by side they have both lanes fully covered and now race towards me! I am no fortuneteller, but I know how this is going to end, and there is nothing I can do about it. Next to the pavement is a steep drop adjacent to a slope several yards deep. In my ignited anger I continuously honk, signal my lights, and wave my arm in order to somehow convince them to slow down and move over, as any responsible person would do. With the last tidbit of hope, I move all the way to the utmost left and drive as slowly as I can. Naively I squeeze out a mild assumption they will still come to their senses. However, they are – and excuse my choice of words but there is no other way of putting it – really that stupid. The passing lorry slams into the widest part of my motorcycle causing me to be thrown off the pavement right down the slope. I've been hit! While I'm still under my bike in the dirt at the bottom of the gully having tumbled down, I notice the truck actually slows down to stop. "So you *do* have a break?" I say aloud in a rhetorical manner. Seeing the driver stop gives me enough strength to crawl from underneath the iron, for I am furious. Stumbling up the slope, I take my helmet off while the driver carefully observes the situation from a safe distance, having stepped out from his vehicle. With blood-red eyes and an outstretched arm, I yell: "You! Stay there!" I run as fast as a bull towards a red cape, determined to smash his skull in with my helmet. The man sees how enraged I am and quickly climbs back into the cabin. When I'm almost there I reach for the door, but he is in his seat by now and puts the pedal to the metal and beats me to the punch. "Come back you coward!" I yell from the top of my lungs. Yet he vanishes, leaving behind a trail of dust and black exhaust fumes.

I can honestly say that if that moron had not gotten away in time, I would have kept beating him until the life would have drained out from his eye sockets. In hindsight, and even up until today, I thank God for letting him get away. Because in all my life this is the closest I got to actually killing another human being, and I know I would have done it at that particular moment. It would have been the straw that broke the camel's back, so to speak, for all those months of frustration prior to this.

Boiling from adrenaline, I keep on driving until it almost gets dark. At a truckers pitch alongside the road are some beds. They are only about five and a half feet, making my own feet stick out. Oh well, at least they are free of charge for a change. Due to the sleepless night from the night before and a long exhausting day on the bike, I fall sound asleep, almost until the next morning. That is quite remarkable because transport and freight traffic continues all night, at a distance of a mere decameter. Yes, including the honking.

Frequent showers are handing out small escapes from the terrible dust but the overall pollution stays the same. Gas stations are scarce, forcing me to anticipate the route. Random villages hold the best opportunities to fill up the bike after having asked around. Often they keep the gasoline in improvised containers such as slurry tanks. Sporadically I am entertained by groups of gathered locals. I reckon they must be sikhs, wearing turbans on their heads in various colors, yet all of them soothing. Slowly but steadily, country roads are changing into multiple lane highways. Tires keep rolling continuously until huge signs appear above the road that makes me sigh: New Delhi! Being so near I sense a type of new energy flowing into me. Massive colonial palaces and genius structures with historical value such as the Red Fort adorn the surroundings. Alternatively, how about the holiest place of the entire subcontinent, the Lotus Temple? A thirty-five-meter-high complex in the shape of a flower. This so-called house of worship holds a capacity to house two and a half thousand people. Surely, one of the reasons why it is so famous is the fact that it is open to all religions. Well almost all because you are not allowed entry with your shoes still on. And it just so happens that fundamental Christianity, with exception of the traditional Roman Catholic branch perhaps, doesn't allow one to take your shoes off to a different god other than YHWH. Before drifting off I must admit, it remains a remarkable piece of engineering without question.

Road signs pointing towards the city center eventually lead to the famous roundabout with indisputable British architecture, the indispensable historic India Gate. One of the biggest and well-known war monuments. After circling the place, I park my two-wheeled transportation next to a patch of intense green grass. Curious kids surround me while a friendly police officer snaps pictures with my camera. While chilling on the curve in glorious sunshine the realization kicks in that I have travelled here all the way over land like the traders from the distant past. Following in the footsteps of the old explorers even. Meanwhile wealthy tourists, dressed in those typical snobby khaki outfits, airy, lightweight and overpriced, pass by in slow-motion. Resentfully looking at my worn out clothes covered in stains.

My ungroomed hair that by now almost reaches my shoulders seems to boggle them even more. I throw them a big provocative smile.

Still, a shower for a change would be nice. Judging from the dirt in my pores the idea is not redundant either. Aimlessly driving around in search for an affordable place to stay I spot a business card on the ground, from the YWCA. When the address on the card turns out to be true, the lady at the reception desk, wearing long black braids, is not fond of my vagabond look. Moreover, in a building loaded with young girls she knows I am like a fox in a hen house. Hunting season has started!

Right in the heart of India and I'm staring at pictures on the wall of Amsterdam, tulips and queen Beatrix. Having made it through the big steel front gate, guards usher me to the waiting room of the Dutch Embassy, where I await my appointment. About five weeks ago I applied for a second passport at the Dutch Consulate in Nepal and now I can pick it up. I will be needing a second one for reasons I'll explain later. A tall suited man equipped with neatly parted hair and golden framed glasses on his nose, takes me to a separate room. He has some questions about my new ID. Compared to the one I have, the signatures are not even remotely similar and I'm baffled by how much the picture differs. To put it this way – if I were standing in his shoes I would have never handed out the new document. My face and haircut appear totally different, but especially the look in my eyes. It is completely unrecognizable from how I looked before. The more I look at it the happier I get. I like this new me. My travels have made me grow so much, igniting a turning point in my life. I feel confident in this confirmation that I am no longer the same person.

Back at the hostel I meet the only other guy that stays there. His name is Brian Cousins and he grew up in Australia. With ginger hair, an allied beard and a wide contagious smile, this crazy musician has been living for months in a basic hidden away town in the northern heights of India. Assimilating with the locals he took it upon himself to learn the *dhol*, the traditional drums of India. Talented as he is, he also perfectly masters the narcotizing harmonium. Hearing this guy perform is an absolute inspiration. Even more so watching how he fully goes up in a passionate kind of way, donating his moves and golden fingers to his dedication. No wonder he ends up later in life as one of the professional pianists of the Australian Ballet. Talking about our lives, we discover that we have been living pretty much the exact same ones at the other sides of this vast world, hence becoming inseparable until time requires to part again.

Roaming the city in a rickshaw, which is a bicycle taxi to the layman, more stimulus follows. We pass security guards in front of banks with huge double-barrelled hunting rifles of about four feet long. I bet the old leftovers from the British Empire do not even work anymore, surely it looks more impressive than threatening. When visiting a cinema with unchanged interior since the twenties, I realize that I cannot take the Bollywood movies serious. One-moment two guys on screen are beating the shit out of each other, next moment they are all singing a song together with choreographed dances and happy faces, only to continue what they were doing. This has to be for a specific kind of audience.

To withdraw from the city's brimming atmosphere, we agree to visit a peaceful fenced park. Disembarking at the entrance we hope to innocently converse without the constant disturbs of the capital's bee hive. It is here where our self-control is put to the test yet another time. In spite of having to pay the mandatory five rupees, the local residents freely enter through the gate. Foreigners such as ourselves are to pay a scandalous sum of twenty-five times more! I understand the business model but this is just plain robbery. What makes them think I have so much money? I am not even employed! Treated with injustice we find out the hard way. Unwittingly we stroll about when we are held standing by a uniformed guard that prevents our entry. Not to be intentionally disrespectful but literally everyone is out to empty my pockets, so I keep on walking to see what happens. When Brian decides to join me due to the ridiculous demand, we are suddenly surrounded by staff of the park who are now threatening to call the police. Reckon it balls of steel or plain stupidity, but I cannot control myself snaring, "Yeah you do that!" The park entertained us only for a while, yet already a man draws near, mentioning he has to speak to us. Lifting up his shirt, his badge reveals that he is from the Indian Secret Service. Brian's countenance turns paler than his light skin already is. We both fear it is bye bye holiday and hello jail time, or worse. To our amazement, the agent had been watching us all along. Against all odds, he starts complimenting our former actions at the entrance. His conclusion is the same as ours; the establishments' rules are bad for tourism. He even promises to get an article in the newspaper about it that very same day. I am certainly no Einstein myself, but finally, we meet the first person with a brain larger than a peanut.

Switching hostels on account of wanting some variety I go from the YWCA to the IYH. Here I meet highly educated Pakistani's for the first time in my life. Moreover, I learn about their intense hate towards Indians and the other way around. Not meaning to generalize here but after meeting dozens more, it is safe to say that this is the overall viewpoint of the situation. Brian persuades me to come over to his new dwelling, the YMCA. There is no need to push me as he mentions that this hostel is in possession of an actual massage salon. It also has better prices, a pool and washing machines. Being able to do laundry is something that comes in mighty handy due to the next small crisis. Brian is so fixated on his breakfast that while shaking the bottle of ketchup he totally fails to realize that the cap was not on. By the time he looks up it is dripping from the ceiling. Pretty much everything on and around our table is covered in blobs of the red sauce, including my face and shirt. An eerie silence follows where he looks startled for a second. Of course, we crack up and can't stop laughing afterwards. The whole restaurant is watching in disgust. However, the funniest thing is, in this total catastrophic mess there isn't even a single spot on him! He is as clean as a nun's underpants on a Sunday morning. Cheers to this remarkable character!

Somewhere in the streets I have my motorcycle fixed for a nickel and a dime. While mechanics are welding, soldering, smashing and screwing unattainable parts together I am reminded of that massage salon at the hostel we're staying at. I feel more or less seduced by the girl in front of the salon, who is definitely easy on the eyes. For days I have been trying to avoid her seducing gaze. Because the flesh is weak, her long lashes finally won me over today. Going inside to make an appointment, she says she has time. After the payment the finely shaped girl directs me to a small room in the back where I need to strip fully naked, only to wear a linen thong. Somewhat uncomfortable I place myself on the stretcher to prepare for the much-anticipated action. Fantasies running freely in my mind. Boy oh boy am I in for a surprise. Little sexy is nowhere to be found when an obvious homosexual walks in and starts pouring a tidal wave of hot oil all over me. To make things worse his hands are hardly pressing the skin. Instead of a firm rub I receive some ritual caressing or something of the like. Presumably turning him on it turns my day into one big fiasco. By the end of the session, I feel more humiliated and battered than deceived. Fleeing the shameful scene, I pack my belongings and check out from the hostel. Convincing myself I nearly escaped this possible rape attempt.

When the Monsoon is not flooding the streets with half a foot of murky water, it is quite nice, and really warm. With increasing riots throughout the big city, the hostile environment increases daily. For that reason plans are brewed to explore other places. Police cars patrol the neighborhood, complete barriers are set up and ropes are tightened between lampposts. Multitudes of protests and demonstrations are in full swing with banners filling the already crowded streets. You can hear the collective shouting from blocks away with loud slogans exiting several bullhorns. With synchronized voices, they march as if their lives depended on it. And maybe that's the case since persecuted women are fighting for their rights, and seas of neglected handicapped people demand a better health care system. Some are throwing objects at the beret wearing police and some are starting a fight. Amidst the chaos, a crippled man throws one of his crutches against a front window of a city bus. He appears to be very angry. Another uses one of his crutches to try to beat up an officer. He instantly regrets it for the officers are all wearing sticks themselves. Heavy-handed they almost beat him healed.

All these things are a good reason to leave the tumult behind. With this choice comes the side effect of having to welcome more suffering. I find myself back to tattered tracks as paved roads belong to the past now. After just a few kilometers, I am immediately overwhelmed by the rummage, the dirt, sand gnashing between my teeth and hideous concrete apartment blocks. Highly underestimated is the imminent over population. Calamitous poverty drives people rigorously mad, so much so that some started selling their organs for a meager remuneration. If you think *they* are having a bad day, in some worse cases they also sell somebody else's organs. Kidneys, lungs, thyroids, you name it. If you have two of something that means you can miss one of those. Then there is the poignant case of children who are sent off to the markets and bus stations with deliberately amputated limbs to gain more compassion from tourists when they beg. We live in a sick world, don't we? Like the great King Solomon once said: "He who increases knowledge, increases sorrow."

Alongside the road are dozens of miles of sprawling Hemp plants, in fact hundreds of miles. Born and raised in the Netherlands I already thought I smelled something familiar. The humid climate is the perfect condition for it to grow, and growing it does. If they only knew how lucrative it can be to sell and export those. Unending roadworks make the traffic even more chaotic than it already is. Most of the time my bike is slim enough to divert the many obstacles. With hundred and four degrees Fahrenheit my uncovered arms simmer tender and are well done. Due to my gloves, my hands remain white, which looks ridiculous in comparison with the rest of my skin, tanned like a retired Fort Lauderdale resident. Via the way of Ambala I end up in Chandigarh, where it turns out that arriving during the ritualistic season of Raksha Bandhan is not the wisest thing I have done. There is just no way of getting used to the disorder and human density. So I am not sticking around here. My motorcycle is performing okay for once so I keep on moving until I reach Amritsar in the afternoon of the next day. You are correct if the name of this large city rings a bell. Nothing less than the world renowned Harmandir Sahib anchors in this city, the religious retreat lasting for six centuries already, better known as the Golden Temple. Accessible through four gates at earth's quarters the sanctuary is surrounded by a pool-like lake called Sarovar. It is the most holy place in Sikhism, and straight away there is a different vibe to the place where zero traces of Hinduism are found. There are an overrepresented number of men in the streets, recognizable with turban and long beards, and hardly any women in public, for they are homebound. When I walk through the back alleys and sandy narrow paths between houses with crumbling wall plaster, I discover the skittish women clustered together, nearly all of them veiled up with a polyester hijab. Without insinuating anything beyond similarities in culture, I think it is no wonder they live in peace with the Islamic community here. In an area with tens of thousands around it amazes me that I am the only white guy, well at least from my perspective I can't detect any other. It makes me wonder what the majority does for a living. Because that same majority does not seem all too occupied with anything. Except for luring gurus and continuously being stared at, I am left alone. Pilgrims from all over Punjab and of course the rest of the country marvel at the white towers, and all the gold and marble.

When evening starts I have a clear view from the hallway on the fifth floor of my hotel. In the jumble of spirituality one thing becomes certain. When the moon rises four times the size of the biggest super moon ever, which actually freaks me out for a while thinking this could be the last night on earth, you know there is some great divine power at work here. Up until now it is the most intense natural phenomenon concerning the celestial bodies I witnessed. For sure the scariest.

With no other Westerners present communication is slow these days. Something as simple as having a conversation can greatly lift spirits. Having tried out several expensive hotels, my mood discerns that the road is calling again. Apparently, I have not yet mastered to fully enjoy where I am. Instead of truly being in the moment and letting go of all fear I put too much pressure on myself trying to get to the next destination. Leaving the comfort of a fan-cooled room behind it is immediately distinctly hot. This region has all the characteristics of a desert. As there is hardly any agriculture around it's landlocked in sand. Back in New Delhi I had already obtained a visa in my passport for the next country I'm going to. Making my way to the border I get excited about the concealed treasures of the inadvisable lands of Pakistan. Little did I know that this day holds nothing but misery in store for me.

When you think about it, it is quite exceptional for a border that stretches thousands of kilometers to have but one border crossing. In this particular case the Wagha border. Standing at one of the windows inside the immigration office the slow pace of uniformed employees increase the tension until they finally stamp my passport. *Was that so hard*, I think to myself, being more impatient than usual. Having packed my gear I slowly drive on a track of no man's land, relieved to be out of India. There I go as a free man towards the big green gates of the Islamic Republic of Pakistan. I cannot wait to move up north to greet the Himalayans one last time. From there I have the adventurous plan to drive all the way to the Middle East. Daydreaming about what's to come is interrupted with the sound of a thousand charging grizzlies, suddenly coming from behind. I am lost for words when the Indian Army comes speeding up with vehicles and half a platoon, just to violently arrest me. Overwhelmed by the volume of force, I am easily overpowered and stand no match. Against my will, I am hurled back into the office I was at before. Armed military staff force me to hand over my passport and since I have absolutely no idea what is about to happen I comply. One of the higher ranked men takes out a pen and puts a cross through my stamp, and writes *Exit Cancelled* beneath it. Obviously bewildered by the situation I begin to realize that I am being denied from exiting the country, so I explode. Now I am shouting at several close-by people, before an unorganized group of camouflaged uniforms starts yelling back at me! For minutes, the office displays a verbalized standoff. No matter how hard I try, no matter how loud I raise my voice in the heat of the moment, without any explanation, I'm being blown off. The fact no one seems to speak English is not helping either. The only two words I do recognize are not very promising. They are: "You!" and "Prison!" An Indian prison is the last thing I want to end up in right now, or ever for that matter. There is nothing left to do than to pack my stuff and find another purpose for the next months. I am devastated.

My new impetuous intentions to make it all the way to the Mediterranean from here crumble to pieces before my eyes. Although it was never a big dream of mine, rather just an infatuation, it seemed like so much more fun than taking an airliner. Now all of the many reflections I had about the great Silk Route are brutally taken from me, such as visiting a Dutch army base in Afghanistan or climbing that lonely monolithic mountain south of the Caspian Sea in Iran. I need some time to let it all sink in. A few hectometers back a colored parasol provides shade in the blistering midday heat. Quenching my thirst with a cold bottle of Mirinda soda, the only soda known to these parts. This orange beverage is so sweet that it makes your teeth rot out while you're drinking it. While feeling defeated I am thinking about my next move with hands in my hair, still embedded in disbelief I bend over in a white chair, when a man with a black mustache also grabs a chair and joins my table. Sitting there in a tank top the unavoidable heat made him remove his striped button shirt. Around his hairy wrist, he is wearing a gold bracelet. Of course, ninety-nine percent of the whole country has a black mustache, but not all of them spontaneously invite me to their home, like this one does. Just like that I find myself a place to crash for the night in a town rather avoided.

Mister mustache and I talk the whole afternoon just sitting at that round plastic table. Then an unusual and intriguing thing happens that makes me say, "I'll take a rain check on that one!" to my new dinner companion. What the hell is happening here? From every angle in the desert, people are moving towards the border in large numbers. My attention is especially drawn to the fact they are all passing the immigration office. When they shuffle towards the area where I was arrested I think I might be dreaming. Dying to know what the fuss is about I blend in to the stream of spectators moving forward with strong current. I'll be damned, large dark green bleachers are set up right in front of Pakistani soil. Sitting themselves down they all seem to be in a cheerful mood. About a staggering five thousand men in total, including women and children. Loud music is stirring up the crowd with people on this side of the fence flapping huge national flags. Through the bars on the other side, I see them waving Pakistani flags from in between the minarets and high towers with the crescent moon on top. Like in a seventeenth century painting, pink crepuscular rays are filling the sky. The patriots show zero restraint, flaunting their nationalism in all sorts of ways. My astonishment rises when the entire crowd sounds as one, howling: "Hindustan! Hindustan!" Which, of course, was the country's name before the British changed it to India. Speaking about the British, during the independence of 1947 they drew the notorious Radcliffe Line straight through the city, dividing it in an eastern part and western part. This phenomenon is often referred to as the Asian Berlin Wall. Military parades of both countries that follow are truly a show to watch. Perfect march and gun movements of the soldiers are very impressive. They began closing the ceremony after a while with the sound of trumpets playing while the flags on either side are lowered at the same time, taken off from the flagpole, neatly folded and handed over to the rivaling country. The time and effort they put into this is nothing less than admirable. Especially because this is done every single day again, at sundown.

Returning to my bike the man is still chilling beneath the parasol in his tank top, sipping his third glass bottle of Mirinda soda as if his gums are immune to the sugar overdose. He assures me that his offer still counts. As he mounts his somewhat emasculated moped, I tail him to his house, where I fall from one surprise into the other. Having my bike and his vehicle stored behind an iron fence, he reveals his house. By far the biggest and most luxurious of the entire remote area. This intriguing figure takes me on a sightseeing walk around the village. Alternatively, should I say *his* village since he owns several shops to begin with. It must be comical for others to see, him as the Don and me as his foreign trophy. Talking has reduced to mere whispers. I would say at least half of all the townspeople are either staring from their stands or following us through the dusty unpaved streets. You know it wouldn't surprise me if I were the first white guy in the whole wide region, ever since the British left sixty years ago.

At night we eat rice and chicken from big platters with his family members. That is to say the male members only. I do get to see the women and girls for a brief moment, his daughters and nieces, before they are safely tucked away again. Close to midnight, things get weird as the men end up in a heated debate because of me. Since they had asked me about my future plans and I candidly mentioned I might be going to visit Israel soon. Without taking time to breathe, they start expressing their hatred towards the Middle Eastern democracy, it seems like it struck a sensitive cord with them. They even demand me to skip it and go straight back to the Netherlands where then I can invite all of them to come over. What kind of intentions could they possibly have? Understandingly I begin to wonder if this isn't some radical Islamic bulwark. I hope that my head will remain on my torso until the next day. I really like it there you know. My head, attached to my torso.

For reasons I think you can understand I am not too sorrowful when our ways part in the morning. I know it is probably just me finding their behavior just a wee bit too suspicious, let alone them owning the only extravagant house around.

So where off to now you might wonder? Well, something about being resourceful. Believe it or not but I'm actually on my way back to the border again, pushing my luck. In my defense, I heard that stubbornness runs in my family. Maybe today there is a different set of staff from the day before? In my mind it's worth giving a shot. Boldly standing at one of the windows again inside the immigration office it is hard to control my nerves. If they catch me now I'm facing possible time where I can't bend over to pick up the bar of soap, so to speak. Judging from the feeling of my face, that does not feel red or insecure; I am doing a good job. Indeed, I recognize no one from the previous day. If all goes according to plan this is going to succeed and will be the most epic thing I have ever done! For a moment, Customs are puzzled when they see the handwritten text in my legal document, making me sweat for a moment from the inlets on my forehead, though everything points toward getting a new stamp after all. Then without any warning it becomes evident that I was rejoicing prematurely. How is it possible? The exact same high-ranking officer that threatened me yesterday comes running toward me with a fresh group of camouflaged soldiers right behind him! Already pointing me out he is shouting something that is probably some kind of order to detain me. In the twinkling of an eye, I snatch my passport back, jump over the barrier and run out from the building. Like a maniac, I spurt away almost feeling their panting on my neck. There is no time to even put on my helmet. With my heart pounding in my chest and admittedly a wet butt crack, I escape from a situation that could have ended much differently. They never caught me and until this day I never know why I was treated the way I was by those acrimonious bobbleheads.

Not to take anything away from its splendor but I feel no desire to visit the Taj Mahal. Rightfully belonging to the newly chosen Seven Wonders of the World, it is too touristy for my taste. I am more attracted to the unexplored. What I *am* searching for is a way to enter Pakistan illegally. Many hours are spent diligently seeking a hole in the fence big enough for my bike and I. After biting the dust I find nothing except a disappointing conclusion; for now, I have to let this one go.

Driving south I stumble upon a massive pile of dead cows, it could easily be hundreds. This produces a grotesque stench that winds carry all throughout the desert. If they are the remains of BSE (mad cow disease) or some weird religious slaughter festival I do not know. There is actually more of these piles scattered about. It's a challenge to not vomit your guts out right away. More nasty smells are met with the finding of a dead camel not too far from the road. Still intact, it cannot be there longer than two days tops. A pack of wild dogs won't let me near it though, they're just sinking their teeth in the carcass. Luckily, the rest of the camels I come across are alive and kicking, and I spot them by the hundreds.

In the maze of the city Ganganagar I get lost instantly. While having a small break at a mechanic to pump air into my tires, I am shown the right directions. According to my roadmap, I now stand at the base of the eight-hundred-kilometer long Rajasthan Desert. A limited bundle of simple food is in my backpack, together with a few bottles of water tied on the back, the only ration I possess. No navigation, no GPS, just a compass and a will to survive. Supposedly a barren wasteland with danger of wild animals and robbers. With my yearning to explore I guess I have been in tougher scrapes before. There I go, against all dissuasions, by myself into the unknown nothingness. Irresponsible as it may seem to some – this is living. Besides, where else do I need to go? The sensation of liberty is unsurpassed. Backpacking the world in extreme ways. Eating new things, learning first hand from other cultures, enjoying not having to work while at the same time growing as a human being. What a wonderful careless life this combination is. You see, this is something to look back on when you're old, not having to regret so much time wasted on useless things.

When traversing the sands I sometimes sleep in crumbling little buildings, long abandoned. One of these nightly shelters is right next to a single train track, in fact one of the few, cutting straight through the despondency. In the black of night when I am sound asleep a monster of a train comes roaring by, totally unexpected, instantly waking me up. Assuming the rail track was not used anymore it almost makes me shit my own pants! At a distance of only three feet away, the ground trembles severely. Fully convinced I am going to die I do not recall ever being so frightened.

Apart from sand flies other nights are far more relaxed. Lying next to cactuses with my sleeping bag zipped open I watch the lighting in the clouds, dozens of miles away across the endless plain. Whereas other deserts can be as dry as a very elderly prostitute, in this one it's not uncommon to be surprised by flash floods. If I don't want to drown in a horrific way, I better pay close attention where I set up camp. During the day I'm easily satisfied with one hundred twenty-five degrees Fahrenheit. For some reason I can handle it very well. Seldom a lorry comes passing by or from the opposite direction, mostly the road is mine. Saturating my eyes with the simplistic beauties of nature, lo and behold on the right side something appears that the mind can hardly comprehend. It is a massive storage facility of all kinds of army vehicles. Tanks, trucks, rocket launchers, everything is there. Impressive for sure, perhaps more concerning than impressive is when I witness this continuing until forever. I mean I count at least a distressing twenty kilometers of unending brand-new war equipment! In addition, an incredible amount of old laid off Soviet junk. Someone is secretly preparing for global decimation, if you let me use that expression. The things you discover while traveling the world eh?

For the first time crossing its borders India knows how to touch me. Its specialty being a beacon of light in the darkness, the blue painted city of mystical Jodhpur. In these dry ongoing flat lands, marked by perspective, it is noticeable from a distance. All the walls of the houses are brushed with an intense blue. Nowadays it is well maintained to keep tourism flowing. In its remoteness it is one of the few means to generate an income, but centuries ago it showed which tribe you belonged to. There is plenty of maize and rice in this old mercantile city, being on the route of the ancient Silk Route. My much-needed supper exists out of just that, filling up my mostly empty stomach. Not that I am not hungry, I just don't allow myself to eat properly. And to be honest it's kinda hard to find something that tastes good, something I did not expect from the country famous for its spices. There are plenty of stands around, but it's not as if I can prepare seeds and things when not having my own kitchen. Strolling towards the old parts, I pass the Umaid Bhavan Palace, erected with marble and sandstone. Locals wearing colorful turbans play annoying melodies on their flutes. Hoping for a tip big enough to feed their families. Avoiding the noise from making ears shrink like a salted snail I aim for higher ground. You cannot miss it, the colossal time-honored Mehrangarh Fort, founded on correlative colored underlying rocks. Proud and monumental with forty-meter high walls, huge arching gates, extended towers, many canons and other anti-siege weapons. The skillful designs are awe inspiring, along with the sunset from the summit over the barren desert, as far as the eye can see. Also, here's the nerdy fun fact of today, it's also the place of this amazing scene where Batman crawls out from that well, escaping by climbing up from the underground tunnel, having been put there by super villain Bane.

Not too far south of this is yet another point of interest. Of course, it's also on the UNESCO World Heritage List, beating you to the punch, because not many people have heard about the Great Wall of India. Yes, you heard it right! Stretching over a length of eighty kilometers this massive well-preserved complex elegantly serpentines through the dry hills. In protection of the adjacent Kumbhalgarh Fort with its dainty yet complicated architecture. Partially constructed with semi bulges sticking out with arched battlements on top. These contain a narrow slit for shooting arrows while at the same time keeping the bowmen safe. It is just wonderful and all pleasing to the eye. This might very well be one of the most hidden man-made structures in the world. I mean for one I had no idea it existed. Therefore, even now in high season when it should be crawling with tourists there are zero westerners to be found, and hardly any folks at all.

Weather nowadays mostly consists of scorching heat alternated with heavy showers. Gradually the heat makes way for humidity. Approaching a sub-tropical climate not much time passes until green trees are back in the game, soon overflowing everything with vegetation and lushness. Long days on the road are the cause of aching joints and bones, especially my knees and bottom. Driving so much on an uncomfortable dirt bike with little food cannot be healthy. Yet I press on. Increasing traffic herald more frequently appearing cities, usually big chaotic ones with horrible roads. Getting nearer to where I am heading the Golf of Khambat is already to my right, which is the west, coming from the north. Faster than anticipated and of course pretty exhausted I arrive late in the afternoon in the financial capital. Surrounded by water this is the unimaginable thicket of Mumbai.

Deep fried food, extremely spicy food, disgusting food, everything is here except a decent meal. Most of the time I have seriously no idea what I am eating. Perhaps there are other things to be concerned about, more important things such as the bombings at the train station where several carriages are blown up, killing over two hundred and injuring around seven hundred! Luckily, I still only travel with my own vehicle, otherwise this trip could have ended very ugly, and this book would not have made it beyond this chapter. Thank God, I am spared of such misfortune. With millions of inhabitants this rising metropolis is too big to effect other parts of it.

Formerly known as Bombay the city is clearly working hard on her reputation. The progressive youth disconnects with older generations, wearing brand clothes and driving fancy motorcycles. Outward appearance is key in this ever-booming economy. Differences in rich and poor is an increasing gap, which is visibly getting worse. This may surprise you but at night even the common areas downtown are worsening every year. Life in the slums is devastating beyond repair, indigestible as it may sound, however the edges of the agglomeration are the worst. Prices of simple hotels are insanely expensive while hundreds of homeless people, more like thousands, are filling up the sidewalks. Laying underneath unfurled cardboard boxes on the heavily polluted tiles. Rats nibbling small pieces of caked waste from bare feet. Now that's an image that will stick in my head for a lifetime. I experience more disbelief when I literally have to step over a surplus of displaced people; there is no end to this madness. My heart breaks by the sight of it and there is nothing I can do. Unfortunately, the Indian government is not doing a darn thing about it either. Wherever you turn your eye, streets are litter-invested with a mixture of mud, dirt and plastic.

It takes a while before I find a place to sleep myself, here and there I get sent away. Some hotels have signs that read "Forbidden for whites!" In other hotels they are less expressive of why I am not welcome. Even when money is shown they make it obvious the reason for refusing me is that they're not fond of my skin color. It might be because of what happened three generations ago, but what does that have to do with me? Discrimination is something I can't comprehend.

Still, it might be better than being a woman in India. A group that are being mistreated on a large and neglected scale. They are beaten, raped, killed, mutilated and burned alive by sick men. Many households have small kerosene ovens that are used to stage an accident. Therefore, it is no exception to see women with horrible burn marks, and so perpetrators often go unpunished. Do not get me started on their version of marriage either, as grooms request disproportionate dowries from their in-law families, who are traditionally obligated to pay for the whole ceremony. Towards the slums, people resemble walking skeletons with sunken eyes and sometimes not too far from decent apartment complexes and neat districts. At those places, it's the Asian Middle Ages right there. Invested with flies, rats, cockroaches and God knows what. Certain shorelines have so much plastic piled up you cannot even see the beach anymore. The water is severely contaminated. I will be the last to point at someone with my finger, yet here it is easy to imagine how those infamous massive islands of rubbish came to be, that are floating across our oceans.

At night a truck saunters brickless streets. Corpses are thrown in the open back of those having lost the struggle against these inhumane conditions. Once your retina testifies of seeing these things, I guarantee you will never be the same person again. I guess the popular travel magazines remain silent about these things, the true life of India. All this while the government is spending billions trying to send a rocket into space which will never make it there anyway. Speaking about a waste of money.

Today I'm watching red crabs at a bayside enjoying the optical illusion of a smaller getting sun. In one of the better neighborhoods, the milled rocks where the little salty creatures hide when disturbed, are still warm from the nice day. Here I am thinking about my time that has come to an end. I would like to drive further to tropical Goa, or even all the way down south to Sri Lanka, but my Jialing motorcycle already fell apart by just watching it. Frankly, I am too sapped to move on like this anyway. Therefore, with pain in my heart, now feeling completely naked and vulnerable again, I just sold that two-wheeled Chinese piece of junk. Due to missing license plates I had to use a fake ID required for the transfer. Luckily for me these jackasses actually fell for my tinker skills, so I guess what I learned from falsifying my bus pass as a teenager came in handy. Finally, a chance to scam somebody back, as I'm still having to face their attempts daily. Remembering the adventure with Steve and beautiful moments with inspiring people, I realize what an incredible journey it has been.

My last days in the country are spent on the exploited and overrated Elephanta Island. No idea about the legitimacy of these things, from what I can see it surely is good for pulling multitudes of tourists to watch the supposed fifth century temples in a cave. No cameras allowed unless you put down additional cash. Everything is about the cash. Walking towards the main attraction the gentle stairs is filled with pushy salesmen and beggars. Their unambitious behavior seems lower than that of the monkeys, which you should also keep an eye on. Once they are done swerving the lianas they will come for you. On the majority of products, a steady selling prize is printed on the wrapper. Regulated by the government you can check what the actual price of products are. Without any shame vendors are asking numbers well above what is legal, not knowing or not caring, they are biting the hand that feeds them. On the ferry towards the island, they charge extra to sit on the upper deck. It seems like they are really making an effort to spoil the mood. Since it remains empty above and crowded as heck below I don't see any point in doing that anyway. I am sure in ten years from now they will even be charging the air you breathe.

It's a small relief when we return to the pier and get out from the mild waves. Boats are unnatural to me. Close to the water, the quayside is graced with the luxurious Taj Mahal Palace hotel, by all means a fascinating structure. Finely tuned architecture is responsible for drawing wealthy Europeans back in the days. In fact, that is the sole reason why it was built for. In more recent times it has also been immensely popular among stars and celebrities. Later on, regrettably, it has been the target of international terrorism as you might remember from the news. A heavily armed and well-trained team of extremists coming from the neighboring country Pakistan, decided to storm the place, hold hostages and even set it on fire due to several explosions. Some people just want to see the world burn.

Last but not least there's the frequently visited Gateway of India at the southern harbor. It is written that the heritage was supposed to have a road that connected with the city center to contribute to growing infrastructure, but it was never built due to a lack of financial sponsors. Right before hopping in a taxi towards the airport (where by the way I board the plane as the last passenger literally ten minutes before it takes off due to heavy traffic) I remember my travels with my Jialing and my ten thousand kilometers of unalloyed voyage over land. Not to mention the dozens of thousand of kilometers I already put to my name with trains on this trip alone. Staring at the monument I try to read the inscriptions sharply chiseled into the big brown stones. They are a vague remnant of a royal stopover by King George V and Queen Mary. Now nothing but a symbol of the once so glorious empire, it serves as a synonym for this trip that all good things must come to an end. Not that raping India by forcing labor on its citizens and robbing its resources was a good thing, but you get the point.

Surely this country has many hidden treasures which you will either love or hate. I've met hundreds of backpackers that absolutely adore it. For me, in spite of not making it to tropical Goa or mother Theresa's Calcutta, from what I have seen so far, I.N.D.I.A. truly stands for I-Never-Do-It-Again!

7

THE GAMBIA

It is in the middle of December 2013 when the heavenly vaults above the Netherlands open up. Darkness glooms all around. As early as seven in the morning storms of snow are coming down hard. All night choirs of wind were raging lamenting songs, so it is no wonder that the subzero temperatures have rendered the roads as hazardous and slippery. On the weather channel, they advise civilians not to go outside unless strictly necessary. Perhaps I was a bit overzealous, I am the only one wearing shorts in the airplane I just boarded. I was already receiving puzzling looks from wide eyes at Schiphol airport.

While loosening up the buckle in my seat it remains a true enigma on why they allow us to get into the plane in the first place. For in the next scandalous four hours that follow we are locked up on the runway, trapped like rats. A thick layer of solid ice has made the airplane almost unrecognizable. Occasionally they actually hose the ice from the wings and engines, yet it's to no avail. With only one tiny refreshment, most of the passengers are fighting boredom and restlessness. Not for me though, don't ask me how I did it, but within no time I make friends with the pilots, who give me a little tour through the cockpit and even let me stay up front in one of the pilot's seats! How cool is that? Seeing all those switches and buttons, the child in me awakens. This is how a flight from barely six hours can turn into one of ten hours. When patience is tested the greater is the reward, or so they say. Right before landing we are welcomed from behind the windows by a turquoise coastline and a surplus of tall palm trees to the *Smiling Coast of Africa*.

Like almost everywhere on earth until the four corners, the predominantly poor locals try to make a quick buck, so to speak. Half the airport offers to carry my luggage upon arrival. When I finally give in and grant a well-dressed man to give me a hand he is disappointed to receive Euro coins instead of Dalasi, the local currency. *Well, what else did you expect?* I find myself thinking sarcastically. *I just freaking landed!* A decent tour bus takes me to my resort in a village called Kotu. Astonishingly enough, at the travel agency a deal containing both the plane ticket and the hotel was cheaper than just the flight itself. You can't make this stuff up. I don't know how they do it, but it definitely works for me.

Due to the season the hotel is decorated with lights, wreath, and a Christmas tree. It is always funny to see such deco when it's boiling hot outside. At least for me, being used to the thermometer indicating below zero around this time of year. When the sun slowly turns orange, the hot climate ensures that my socks will stay in my backpack. I won't be needing those. Life cannot get any better chilling beneath a wicker bumbershoot with a dreamy view across the ocean, or can it? The traditional dish of *Domoda* is the first culinary cultural experience I have. It is basically a rich peanut stew and that's as intriguing as it sounds.

In the course of days it becomes apparent that almost everyone is trying to get a piece of the action from the prosperous white devils. Yes, this racially charged description includes me. Nearly all have an arsenal of tricks up their frayed sleeve, some of which I have not seen since the days of David Copperfield. Unfortunately for them, their skills hardly work with me, being a thoroughly seasoned man of the world. Due to my significant number of travels, I became an expert on detecting scams and fraudulent activities, but make no mistake, they are well-trained and not easily brushed off. Now that I am getting older I do admit that I am more prone to their lies. It becomes especially hard when they unleash a battle against your conscience so hereby be forewarned.

Obviously not everyone has a double agenda. On my way to the supermarket, a wooden structure the size of an average lavatory, I meet a gentle hospitable Rastafarian. He takes me to his living environment in the jungle where we talk back and forth until it's evening. Meeting him and his friends ignites several small yet intriguing endeavors. In fact, from this day forward, I end up spending my nights in seedy motels, apartments in unknown places and insect infested jungles. Meeting them causes me to not sleep at my resort any longer.

During our first long conversation, we are accompanied by a large sum of El Hella tea. This is how it is prepared: in total, it is boiled three times. First very bitter, then less bitter (but still disgusting) and last but not least, sweet – partially due to the insane amount of sugar added. Please note that it needs to be consumed in all three stages. Then you pour the steaming liquid from the kettle into a small glass, with a challenging long trickle, prior to repetitively pouring it from one glass into another until a good milky head appears. Soon I learn that you don't barge in here for a quick visit. In Gambian culture a meeting is more often than not time-consuming, to say the least. Hours can turn into a whole day; a day can easily turn into several days. Time is something intangible. During supper with the newly acquainted and a bunch of his friends, we all eat rice and fish from the same round platter. Sharing what you have is quite common among Gambian people and often essential as well. Unlike in India, where you eat with three fingers, you use your whole hand here. A small ball of food is formed in the palm of the hand before licking it out and going for the next round, but be sure not to eat the flies. If you do not constantly chase them away, they are all over your food. I reckon cramps and diarrhea are guaranteed after such meals where you are basically eating each others saliva.

By the time rice expands in our stomachs, the first bag of marihuana emerges. Even during the day, it is hard not to notice that pretty much the entire village has red eyes. I have never seen so many people together that are simultaneously stoned out of their minds. The people refer to their smoke in a comical way, as 'Bob Marley cigarettes'.

Friends of my new friend become my brothers, according to them we are all family. "A brother from another mother!" they say. To make it easy, his brothers who are actually his friends are also his colleagues. On the payroll of a nearby hotel, they are responsible for minor maintenance. For each one individually their professions are printed on the back of their lab coats. Funnily enough these are sponsored by a Dutch supermarket chain.

On one of these days I return for a while to my resort. In my room, I enjoy a long shower and trade my smelly clothes for a set of clean ones. Hotel staff wonder where their guest has been. Before I give them a chance to ask I am already out again. Right before the evening, I meet up with my so-called brothers again in the jungle. I discover that I should take their words with a pinch of salt as they claim to have worked hard all day, yet all they did was move a mattress from one room to another, nearly sixty meters apart. Slouching on their beds with a big fat joint and half-closed eyelids I'm assured they're having a well-deserved rest from the heavy labor. Do not get me wrong, they certainly are kindness personified, but my oh my no wonder there is zero progressiveness.

Just off the beach, sandbanks and breathtaking rock formations are disclosed by the reoccurring low tides of the ocean. A standard of thirty-five degrees Celsius simmers my skin well-done, about two complexions away from possible skin cancer, hence never miss out on sunscreen. Lush wilderness full of plants and animal life are revitalizing. There is an abundance of the sweetest fruits growing in the trees, free for anyone to take, the way nature intended it to be. Big lizards, hawks, eagles, monkeys, vultures, white herons and an excess of never seen before bugs creeping about. In the shades of overgrown streams, it is no surprise to spot bright red crabs, medium size crocodiles and even piranha's, being bigger than you might expect.

On the beach I assist local fishermen just having returned from open water, by untangling their large nets. Consisting of a serious hunk of muscle we pile up freshly caught sharks. An occasional tuna fish or stingray is found between the spoils, but all have to submit to the lack of H2O before they are off to the fish market that I will visit later on.

With my bare feet still standing in the hot sand something else draws my attention. A group of bulky men start exercising on the beach. This is my first encounter with one of the better wrestling teams from the Gambia. Not only do they draw my attention, their attention is drawn to me also, being one of the few white guys showing interest in their sport. From that moment on I am invited to join them and my training starts, which is held once every three days. Soon my muscles ache from the work-outs and my body hurts from the training. They do not hold back in treating me like a rookie or something, every chance they get they smack me to the ground using their raw strength and set of skills. Determined to possess the same skills I receive some one-on-one lessons from the trainer. These sessions definitely pay off, meanwhile I visibly grow in size daily. When it is close to an official match everyone from the team, including me, is subject to wear a traditional outfit. To know that this is nothing more than completely naked with a burlap thong! It is a ridiculous sight. While shooting the promotion video, where we perform a choreographed dance, I am contrastingly lacking in color among the dark-skinned wrestlers, and maybe some body mass too.

Not sure if I have an underdeveloped talent here but during one of the training sessions, weeks later from when I began, I manage to floor one of the professionals. Everyone is impressed but me the most. What a great and unforgettable experience. I will forever be grateful to the team who took me in and treated me as one of their own. Fantastic.

In all fairness, I need not to worry about any difference in pigmentation. The local community accepts me wholeheartedly. The ones seeing me on a regular basis call me by my Gambian name 'Brother Peace' that was somehow bestowed upon me. Other eccentric names I frequently hear are 'Muscleman', 'Tattooman', 'Good Muslim', and last but not least 'Friend of God', which coincidently is the true meaning of my actual name. Although I had no idea whether they actually knew that.

At one point my new brothers convince me to join them to a Rasta party at night. Far removed from my preferable genre we hit the streets with loud Jamaican music in the district of Kololi. Being the only white guy in the crowd it takes some time of getting used to. I mean of course I have something to prove among these people who have an innate feeling for rhythm. Since I wasn't born yesterday I win some credit due to my dance moves. I am not as inflexible as most westerners in my age range. Needless to say, everyone is smoking pot to the limit. Someone from the crowd comes up to me and tells me unexpectedly: "Yah man, it's all love." Pretty much all the locals use the same slogans repeatedly. Other ones often heard are: "Good people meet good people", "It's not easy you know!" or "What is your nice name?" By far the most used, being almost a trade-mark for the region, is: "It's nice to be nice!" This one is my personal favorite because whilst saying it they like to give big smiles and show their insanely white teeth. Those by the way are kept that white without the aid of toothpaste or a toothbrush. Amazingly enough a little twig from a certain tree is used to scrape it all clean and in essence this is all you need. Of course, the big companies in the western world, consumed by making profit instead of caring about health, teach us how to poison ourselves with all sorts of mouth cleaning products full of fluoride. In the end, everything we need is offered by nature.

Together with two blond-haired Dutch girls, we roam the area on rented bicycles. I met them in one of the moments I went to my room to change clothes at the resort. Along the way it is tough not to be bothered by the amount of junk we come across. Plastic of all sorts, wood waste and smelly ponds are everywhere. It's not a secret to how it became such a mess as everyone contributes to it and even before our very eyes. Cycling on an unpaved dirt road we witness a man finishing his plastic bottle of soda and carelessly throwing it aside, even without taking the effort to see where it lands. All he knows is it will blend in with the rest of the rubbish. Back home my government is inexhaustibly pushing civilians for the agenda to separate waste, which most actually do, but seeing all this now, to what end?

More suspicious odors welcome us when we arrive at the Bakau Fish Market, although here this is to be expected. Colorful fishing boats with empty nets and fully ordained women stimulate the senses. Varieties of fish lay exhibited on improvised picket tables next to the bigger stalls. It cannot get any fresher than this. Out of the water straight to the cutting board of the salesmen. Walking in the midst of it all the smell is unbearable in this heat. An army of flies unleash in apocalyptic measures as if a next plague has broken out. Beneath wooden tables lie pieces of intestines, heads, skin and bone, and take my word for it that those pieces have been rotting away for weeks, months and even years. That is a crash course of life in Africa for you.

Some of the children present live in such poverty that we are moved enough to treat them to food and toys. What more can you do, right? When they hug us and do not want to let go we understand it is not because they desire more, for we sense the love and gratefulness they are transmitting, but simply to show thankfulness. Their heartfelt smiles are priceless.

Although bicycle rides are fun, my real quest is to rent a

motorcycle. I would even buy one if I had to. Since I am sort of low on cash I need to get myself a proper deal though. I happen to know a guy that supposedly knows an official store. Having walked at least ten miles in the blistering heat it turns out the official store is comprised of a random stranger that has a brother living in the bush who is willing to give up on his bike. Scratching my chin I sigh a long: "I see…" I'm not eager to accuse anyone of racism, but I highly suspect that the price goes up disproportionally on account of him noticing my skin tone. Well, I ain't falling for that one. Standing with my thumb out for a couple of minutes two ladies in an old Suzuki Vitara are kind enough to bring me back to Kotu. There the search continues. I learn from the same guy I ran into earlier that he has a friend with a Kawasaki 500. This one is promised to be available after fixing some spare parts. However, the deal has too many strings attached so I will not get to ride a motorcycle for my whole time of being here. Too bad. It would be so easy for some of these guys to make decent money. You just have to know how to make it.

Residents invite me to visit their house daily to meet their families. Other tourists seem clocked up in spending their time in loungers at the coast, or even end up wasting their time staying at the pool at their resorts. I cannot get into all the demands and I certainly cannot describe all that takes place, yet the following events are worth mentioning. Starting with something that will remain with me for the rest of my life.

Have you ever heard of *Juju*? Neither did I before coming here. It's a form of black magic that is practiced in a large portion of West Africa and I'm about to undergo the spells of voodoo firsthand. Ending up in a wooden shack of one of my hosts, he shows me a string with beads tied around his upper arm. That's all the power he can handle for now. When certain tribes go to war they tie one of those strings with beads around their waste to gain enormous powers, even shielding themselves with a spiritual layer of protection that apparently make bullets bounce off from their bodies. Of course, my first reaction is:

"Enjoying your LSD so far sir?", kind of ridiculing the situation. I go on asking: "Maybe you have a feverish attack of malaria?", as could very well be the case in this country. Yet nothing can be further from the truth. Grabbing a knife as big as the length of a man's hand, without taking the measurements of the hilt into consideration, he is ready to perform a small demonstration. First, he firmly presses the blade in his hand and arm trying to make a cut. Nothing happens. Then he takes it with both hands and stabs himself in the belly in full force! Again without damaging results nor blood or even the slightest cut! I am standing literally one meter away from him and have a good view. It is hard to believe my own eyes, maybe I am the one having malaria? Now it's time for the scary part. Standing face to face, he places the blade in my right hand and tells me to stab him. "Are you serious?" I stutter but his nod tells me he is. A quick check reveals the edge is razor-sharp. Placing my left hand on his right shoulder for stability, I get ready to do as he ordered. Bending my knees and spreading my legs a little to brace myself for the impact I am about to cause. While I am holding my breath he takes a deep one and then I do it! I can feel my heart pounding in my chest as I try to shank him in his bowels, and again, and again. No matter how I try, the stainless steel cannot seem to penetrate his flesh. Such an act would instantly be lethal to any other human being. I do not know if they found a way to summon demons or something to become as hard as stone, for me, it leaves a bad taste in my mouth for the rest of the day. No doubt it is one of the spookiest experiences of witchcraft I've ever been involved in.

Luckily, not all my hosts are plain weirdos. A man my age that I met on the beach brings me to the market of the district of Serekunda, which is quite something. Once again flies are overrepresented. An enormous amount of fruits, sheets and towels, hardware, spices, fish, you name it. A lot of the commodity comes from French-speaking Senegalese, having a big percentage in trading within this area. Women and girls alike are dressed in prismatic robes and headscarves, sometimes the headscarves even match their robes. In spite of being crowded as heck, the roads are decent and the overall vibe feels safe and friendly.

After this, we head to his home in perhaps the poorest village of the country, bordering one of the arms of the nation's largest river. In Ebo Town the roads solely consist out of sand and dirt, puddles of stinking mud are everywhere. Poorly constructed houses and shacks that are nearly falling apart is the normal state of affairs. All homes are unnumbered and kids seldomly attend school. Something hard to miss is the intensity of their skin, they're not just a bit dark, neither colored or brown skinned, but they are seriously black, contributing to the diversity of this amazing world. No one cares about the nonchalant donkeys, too skinny for western standards, that mindlessly chew the garbage while partially plucked chickens run around; seemingly afraid it might be their last day. Occasionally you hear dogs barking. Speaking about dogs, there is not a single bitch that hasn't got a string of those droopy teats hanging out, as they let nature run its course, without any intervention.

The compound of my host is made up from concrete cubicles with cracked corrugated sheets, while pieces of rebar are jacked in the windowpanes. None of the structures have gutters due to the chronicle absence of rain. Lamin's wife, who is much younger and very beautiful, is preparing a meal in the kitchen. I chuckle as they take the concept of an open space kitchen very literally over here. Fragrances from the fire with pots and pans hanging above it make the whole family on the inner court hungry. When I throw in some of my Mandinka, their tribal language, it seems to amuse everyone. Especially the children, mesmerized by how I look so different from them they are curiously pinching my alabaster skin, at least in comparison, feeling my blond hair and pointing at my blue eyes. They are not letting the chance slip away to touch me and study me. Hence, I find them crawling on my lap, my feet, my shoulders, and the ones incapable of climbing on me are glued to my side. By now I am encompassed by focused glares from a multitude of dark eyes. Uncles, grandmothers and neighbors visit as I am the first foreigner to ever set foot in their compounds, which is absolutely an honor to me as it's a sign that I earned their trust and respect. Relatively often people ask me if it isn't boring to travel by myself. Rest assured, it is precisely by traveling alone that you embrace situations such as this. Some of the younger ones, barely able to walk on their own, look startled and start to cry. For they have truly never seen a white person before. If that doesn't make you feel like one of the seventeenth century explorers, I don't know what will. I have become a living theme park in a place where I wanted to stay incognito.

Meandering the perimeter, we are confronted with harsh living conditions. What reminds me about certain places in Asia is that women will do all the work around here. They have taken the responsibility upon themselves to cook, clean, do the laundry and the groceries, take care of the children, sustain the vegetable garden and a thousand things more, all while their husbands are out smoking weed daily, occasionally hassle tourists pretending to be looking for work. It really is a vicious circle. Therefore, it is pleasing to the soul to be able to provide a little bit of help. For less than the quantity of money I can make in a single day back home I get them provisions. It is hard to carry the huge bags of rice that will easily last for a month for the entire compound. I also try to buy a big piece of fresh fish but they purposely charge too much. Not knowing Lamin and I are there together I give him cash out of sight from the salesman and he gets it anyway. Later that day, one more time going back and forth to the market I get something that's definitely not redundant. Handing over some large thick blankets for them to sleep on, my hosts assure me that a concrete floor is pretty bad for the joints.

As days progress we meet up with an old crippled imam and some friends of his, but the thing that will stick with me for a lifetime is when we reach a milestone of poverty. In the middle of a more or less abandoned street, actually being a dirt road, a young woman comes up to me and delivers her newborn child into my arms. "Take him with you!" she yells as she walks away. Okay. I guess now I am the owner of a brand-new black baby. Imagine being so desperate as a mother that you'll give away your own son! There is a thin line between being irresponsible and simply hoping for a better future for him. One thing is certain, without using contraceptives they are popping out kids that they cannot support. While wondering what to do I keep on going with that baby in my arms until I find someone willing to take care of it. It remains unknown to me if the child was ever returned to its rightful owner.

On my way back to the jungle of Kotu I hit upon a true junkyard. It's definitely the biggest I have ever seen. It is miles and miles in diameter. Pillars of smoke arise from small fires with unbearable scents of burning piles of plastic, melting rubber and murky putrid disposal. Wild cows are chewing rotting waste, magpies fight over crumbs of utter shit, and rats feast upon anything they can possibly find, even on each other if they have to. There's actually quite a few people scouting through the rubbish. Collecting whatever they can find in order to hopefully earn enough money to make it to the next day. A heartbreaking and a worrying sight, and hard to believe too but nowadays it has become so large that it extends all the way to the suburbs and residential areas right next to it. You would not grant these conditions to your worst enemy.

Precisely because of the destituteness all around the country, several foreign nonprofit organizations attempt to provide a helping hand, or so it seems. At the location of one of these organizations, that so happens to be quite a famous branch in Germany and the Netherlands, things seem a bit out of the ordinary. At least I do not see any reason why you would wash fancy Land Rovers all day, instead of feeding orphans, educating children and providing the help you are known and praised for. After inquiring for information and a tour around the compound I'm kindly asked to leave the premises. The craziest thing of all is that I do not see children anywhere, and that is supposed to be the target group. When the Dutch girls from the same resort go there with pencils, balloons, and backpacks full of good intentions they have similar experiences. This raises serious questions about the integrity of people working there, collecting hundreds of thousands of euros through fundraising. If it wasn't for an elderly German woman that I met in Egypt a year prior I might have doubts still. However, she had worked for many of these non-profits throughout the continent of Africa and was shocked by what she discovered. While camping out in the desert for a night I listen closely to all she has to say in the dimming light of the bonfire. Because I had seen the facility with my own eyes, and witnessed the deficiencies thereof first-hand, her claims of ninety-nine percent of them being a total scam was hereby confirmed for me. It even gets so ugly up to the point of them handing out free drugs to the kids, right before some delegation or interest group would visit the place. Now that it seemed most are indeed addicted, the funds will keep coming in. Clever move, but sickening to the core.

Besides meeting the German woman who revealed many shocking details about African non-profit organizations, some more things happened during my stay in Egypt. For one, traveling there in time of war, aka the Arab Spring, I was awarded with visiting the Pyramids of Giza all by myself. This hotspot is normally weighed down under the crawling masses of tourists, yet now it is completely deserted. Imagine that, as if no one in the world had yet explored the ancient wonders. And it did not end there. Later on during that trip I got rejected at the border with Saudi Arabia, followed by a police officer that brought me to his station, close to the Gulf of Aqaba, to try to sell me a humongous bag of marihuana. This not being my field or anything but having seen some weird things when I was younger I would say it had an estimated street value of two hundred thousand dollars at least. If that wasn't enough I met a homosexual over fifty who claimed to have given a blowjob to Elton John back in the days whilst he was touring. Now ask yourself, how often do you meet a person that had the penis of a celebrity in his mouth? To close it off, I received a phone call from a Dutch producer telling me that I made it to the last thirty people of a television show, that I signed up for. Knowing, that I was handpicked from out of four and a half thousand candidates, she basically told me I had a green light to participate in a lengthy reality show with the chances of winning a large sum of cash. After receiving further instructions, I declined because I felt they had lied about the terms and conditions. You are a man of principles or you are not. The moral of this short inserted story about Egypt, is that of all the wondrous things that happened over there, the thing that the elderly German woman told me about the wrongdoings in Africa stuck with me the most. For that reason, I never give anything to charity. It amazes me that no one catches the giant red flags when CEOs of non-profit organizations are driving in hugely expensive cars.

Time is spent meeting people, drinking lots and lots of tea, and of course, no adventure can be vacant from it - with women. I am not talking about the ones you have to pay for in the touristy areas, south of Kotu. Where clubs and bars lure you into an intoxicating nightlife, forcing you to make shady deals, not leaving the country before you have one of the many STD's, or even AIDS. Statistics about these afflictions are absolutely shocking. Unfortunately, nobody is doing a darn thing about it including the government. It seems illegal prostitution is just another way of life. Even if you try to avoid it, you are confronted with it one way or another. Guys approach me in the streets up to several times a day and without shame they ask if I'm interested in a girl. Apparently, they can arrange anything from old to young, and when I don't show interest in payed sex they usually have a spare sister or cousin they try to haggle. If I had responded to all the requests, my dick would have fallen off by now. However, there are others that do respond. With appropriate bias just not the type of people you would first expect.

Whereas in countries like Thailand for instance you can see overweight balding men going out with younger girls, or even very young ones, here the exact opposite is the case. Ugly saggy white women, way passed their expiration date, a lot of them coming from northern European countries, are not in the least way embarrassed to hook up with young boys. Those young black boys with slender bodies always claim to be in their early or mid-twenties. Though it is no exception they are somewhere between fourteen and eighteen. In general, men get the blame for everything but I think we can all agree this is outrageous and should not be allowed. As of yet, this way of extortion and the grooming of children is grossly ignored by the world. In the event that such issues emerge into the limelight, they are instantly nullified and branded as a mere incident. I can assure you this is a false narrative and an ongoing trend to this day. It is truly astonishing to see those kids fucking anything with a heartbeat, or at least anything with the slightest vestige of body heat, with the hope of getting something in return. Twisting the romance of a healthy relationship it is cringeworthy to watch them go hand in hand through the ankle deep billows during sunset, little boys with fat selfish white women with varicose veins that could pass as their grandmothers.

Okay where was I? Right, spending time meeting people, including women. Not far from my resort, I purchase a bowl of delicious fruit on the beach. While enjoying small talk in the shadows of palm trees, the wig wearing stall girl suddenly grabs me by the hand and parades me around. Cunningly, so that everybody can see. Next thing I know I find her tongue in my ear and right after in my mouth. Not that she tries to kiss me, for Gambians do not know how to do that, but just her tongue in the back of my throat. Interestingly, the consequence of that action convinced her that we belong together now. Studying the nation, I think it is safe to conclude their way of thinking is quite primitive when it comes to male-female relationships. The overall behavior is no different than jealous pubescent teen girls. When they have spotted you first you're not allowed to engage in any type of conversation with anyone else. Because of this, for just talking to other girls, I am labelled as a cheater in no time. Unbelievable.

To illustrate this further, the two blond Dutch girls I met are labelled as sluts by everyone I talk to, guys and girls alike. Only because they chat to different guys who upon their turn approach them instead of the other way around. In fact, most of the time it's them getting harassed. Ah well, I suppose 'Life is life you know', as is another one of their infamous tacky slogans.

The real fun starts when I find a handwritten note in my bedroom between my fresh towels from a girl working at the restaurant. Although we only talked once for about three minutes I am glad to find out that she 'misses me'. Besides her, I already have a date with another girl, coincidently from the same restaurant. This one is stunningly gorgeous, and to see her in something else than her waitress uniform is a present I couldn't have asked for. With a shy stroll holding hands in another neighborhood, transients are shouting: "Hey lucky man!" and the envious ones go like "Hey, lucky woman!", wrongly thinking she hit the jackpot or something. Persistently stoned as everyone is, hardly anything escapes anyone's eyes. After some tropical nights on an isolated moonlit beach, she takes me to meet her family in Banjul, the capital of the Gambia. In these communities, the families are usually huge. I could have known this one is no different. Like now as in many times before elsewhere I am one of the few white people to step over the threshold, making it a meeting to remember for both parties.

In the short time I travelled the slim country I met an outlandish amount of people. My unquenchable thirst for the unknown has once more demonstrated that it is hard to say no. However, I'm slowly improving my abilities to not go into everything. A trait that is most necessary for me to learn. You see, in the final days of being in the village of Kotu I realize I had spent all my money on trying to help others. Indeed, it gets so tight I can no longer afford to properly sustain myself. Thus, finding myself at a local refugee center for a few nights. There I stand in line with a plastic plate waiting for a free meal. Oh the irony. Judging from the look on their faces the Christian volunteers have a hard time believing me. Thanks to their big compassionate hearts, they serve me anyway.

Being here due to my predicament it seems as if more good things come out of it. Through a cousin of one of the brothers from the jungle I previously met, I encounter this fine young woman. She is about to go home when we give in to an unresisting instant attraction. Her slim body of forty-five kilograms moves enticingly close to mine, still buffed up from the wrestle training sessions. With natural full lips, long braided hair and dark chocolate skin, she's a real beauty. When her taxi comes rolling by she orders the driver to wait for a minute. With the sound of the engine running in the background, we hide behind a small concrete ledge away from the lights, cutting through the dark, and have some free-spirited sex amidst exuberant vegetation. Not rushed but quick enough for the driver not to grow impatient. That certainly smacks of a summer fling at the last moment. In the next few days, we get to know each other better in a hotel room donated by a mutual friend.

It's here I found out the hard way that she belongs to the Mandinka tribe. Well, the hard way, more like the intriguing way. With my head between her thighs, I conclude that she is missing that one vital part that I was sort of down there for in the first place. Namely, this tribe has the old habit of mutilating the genitalia of their daughters, due to female circumcision she does not have a clitoris anymore, which makes it somewhat impossible to concentrate. Just when you think you have seen it all eh? Literally and figuratively speaking a small reminder of the hidden gruesomeness of the country. Looking at things from a positive perspective, as we would say among men in construction, innocently unaware of any form of sexism, at least the inner tube was just as pink! It's nice to be nice!

8

JORDAN

Little aerodynamically shaped swallows fly ecstatically back and forth. Soon the nippy whiff will turn into warm waves of air. Curious rays of sunshine appear in the early heavens, causing long shadows to fall off the battlements of the old city wall. It's summer in an awakening Jerusalem, becoming more apparent every minute. The small hand of time barely reaches six when, at the Damascus Gate, on the north eastern side, salesmen are setting up their market stalls. Persian rugs are laid on the stone steps, while fresh fruit and new shoes are carelessly placed next to each other. There are strong scents of bread and spices, yet the smells of the triumphant morning prevail.

For the past seven months I've been residing in Israel, in both the capital, on the Mount of Olives, as well as in Jaffa, a cozy harbor town at a walkable distance south of Tel Aviv. I don't have time to get into it now, so hopefully in the next book I can elaborate more on things like the hours-long interrogation upon entry, how I almost got seriously injured by a group of young Palestinian men, my experiences at hostile check posts, disturbing refugee camps, the ancient biblical sites and the exhilarating daily life in poor Ramallah, late Yasser Arafat's city. And of course much more.

For now, the focus is on the present activity: my hike towards the border, armed in white linen and equipped with backpack and a pair of Nordic walking sticks. You're allowed to laugh, I don't care. I happen to like those sticks that give a tremendous support to the body. In any case, when Mother Nature exhumes the battle axe almost immediately the suffering begins. Water is scarce and every green leaf has long been scorched by the increasing heat. Moving forward through loose sand is tiring, as well as hiking through fields of cluttered tennis ball-sized rocks. Once in the dry hills I meet barren places with amber shades. Here I'm getting ambushed by a surprise.

Better yet an intriguing encounter. People had previously warned me against Arabic nomads in the mountains. Tales of individuals that got murdered, never to be found again, are not uncommon. When I stumble upon several Bedouin tents I'm instantly reminded of this. To announce my approach, I call out: *"Merhaba!"* which translates to hello. Children spot me first. Crazy enough their natural response is to quickly gather gravel and start throwing it at me, some of the stones being the size of decent eggs. Using my left arm to protect my face I keep approaching until they realize, with certain hesitation, that I can't be Jewish. Then the adults gather and within moments I'm surrounded by a large portion of the tribe. It is somewhat worrying due to the many violent rumors going about.

Not having a fridge or any type of electricity around I assume they store their reserves underground, when I unexpectedly get handed a tin pan of cold water. Judging from the look on their faces I am not the only one that didn't see that coming. Children are poor and their skin dirty with stains covering their clothing. They point at my wrist watch and try to open my backpack that I placed on the ground. Clever knots I previously made in the strings are preventing that. They have me sit down in the light shadow of a stretched-out cloth when one of the young adults starts to clap his hands. Others follow rapidly and bring self-improvised instruments to the show, putting me at ease. Their new guest, most certainly impressed, is treated to a traditional folk dance of singing nomads! I'm in awe of the unprompted entertainment and get to see the human dimension of this gypsy-like community.

Contrary to daily temperatures the nights are freezing cold. Since a sleeping bag is too much to carry around a small fleece blanket has to do all the heavy work. Once again, I sacrifice comfort for the sake of adventure. In the hours I lie awake at night, by myself in the desert, I survey the stars and try to calculate my location by the different angles of constellations. The silence of long and lonely nights is breached by the distant echoes of bullets whizzing through the pitch black. Often omitted by the media, this war that has already lasted for thousands of years, has never stopped. Daylight invites me to pack my stuff and keep moving. As if the Holy Spirit is guiding my steps I notice a beautiful soft-toned dove constantly following me. But then again it just might be a hungry bird.

In front of the ruins of four-and-a-half-thousand-year-old Jericho I'm held up by a check post, the last one before entering Judea and Samaria, better known as the West Bank. A group of armed Israeli soldiers inquire what the hell I'm doing here by myself on foot. "Well I'm heading east, preferably as far as I can get" is my reply. And that is exactly what I'm doing. After a while I learn they are on high alert, recently having fought against Hezbollah in the north, just below Lebanon. After earning their trust, I receive provisions in the form of fruits and water. Thank you IDF. At our parting a soldier shouts at me from the watchtower: "I will blow away anyone who comes near you!", recklessly swinging his massive machine gun about. I can't help to chuckle. No matter how you feel about the Knesset and the regime in power, it's astonishing that this country is defended by a bunch of teenagers.

Deeper into Palestinian occupied territory the remains of bloody, unceasing disputes from former colonies are reminiscent, with rubble from exploded houses and scattered bullet holes in whatever is left standing. Mine fields are separated from the unpaved main road merely by barbed wire, only the occasional sign strung up with scrap wire warns against this. Once in the city center it seems as if suspicious eyes monitor every movement I make, but I guess I'm no different when it comes to that. Overall it doesn't make a very safe impression.

Late in the afternoon I arrive at the heavily guarded river, which is the border. One of the three crossings to the Kingdom of Jordan is the Allenby Bridge which was constructed on top of the decrepit remains of the Ottoman Empire. This bridge was named after a British general. The gentlemen at Immigration are dumbfounded to find me all by myself with my walking sticks. That's something they don't see every day. And just in case you're wondering yourself what I'm doing here I agree I owe you a small explanation. I decided to explore the Muslim world of the Middle East by making a journey on foot through countries you usually only see on the six o'clock news. I wanted to find out what's really happening in these places that we know so little about. After having my passports thoroughly checked they put me on the last bus for the day, that is seconds away from leaving. I feel honored being the last tourist of today. It's mandatory to take this prearranged bus, as for good reasons it is illegal to cross the border individually.

Upon arrival in the land of King Abdullah the Second, who is a direct descendant of the Prophet Muhammad himself, according to the genealogy on the website of the Jordanian embassy, intrusive taxi drivers are baiting me with sharp prices, in a manner that only Arabs can. However, their skilled rattling is falling on deaf ears. I put my sunglasses on to enjoy the sight of the low orange sun and begin to walk. Thick trunked palm trees make a formal bow as they welcome me on Edomite soil. One can't help but notice the aggravating and unnecessary litter ruining the place. Dust makes my mouth dry and even the air is needy of moisture. At this hour the traffic has diminished to nothing. With absence of occasional passers-by, I manage to fix myself a place to sleep for tonight. Climbing over a fence an unclear path leads to a fig nursery, where it's easy to hide between big, dense leaves. In this private-owned patch of land dogs are frequently snooping around. To prevent their barking from exposing my hiding spot I actually sleep with a knife in my hand. Luckily for both parties the night goes by without any harm done.

It turns out to be a bit of a challenge to get clean drinking water. Here the streets have no name and the houses have no numbers. And to make things worse, crossing through dead-end villages, no living soul speaks English. Alongside the road are rusting cars without tires. Occasional houses I encounter are poorly maintained, if at all. Did you know the amount of roadkill dogs are about the same as the living ones? Literally every single one of the last-mentioned group has an aggressive attitude. Seeing how animals are treated by the locals it comes as no surprise. They're kicked, beaten and shouted at, whilst not receiving love from anyone. If only they knew the joy a pet could bring. At the threshold of the first piece of extended desert that I need to cross, a tiny store allows for cans of orange juice and salty sausage, bursting from garlic. Since this is my last chance to collect some serious ration, I should be stacking my backpack, yet I do not. Without having obtained local currency, due to the lack of ATMs, the handful of exchanged money I carried is now gone, preventing to get properly equipped. Meaning I will be crossing this desolate wasteland entirely on faith. Somehow knowing, instead of hoping, I will be taken care of.

Call it stupidity, call it determination, but there I go in the heat of the day towards a never-ending horizon. Plagued by thirst I pant forward despite my pace slowing down until I drop to my knees. To say that I feel refreshed after a period of rest would be an exaggeration, but I receive just enough energy to get back on my feet to continue. Circling vultures in the sky are paying too much attention to me. Hours pass until a dot appears in the distance. Some more hours pass until I finally reach the dot, now grown into an actual structure. And what do you know? In the middle of nowhere there is this army base. Of course, military staff keeping watch have observed me from far away. Wondering why anyone would solo travel to their compound, let alone survive the desert. Jordanian soldiers who, for reasons unknown, all carry a big mustache, are eager to invite me into their camp. With unsurpassed hospitality I'm received. All the men surrounding me are very interested in my story. While letting me fill up my hydration bladder they are quick to serve ice-cold water, showcasing decency and respect, for they understand, like no one else, I must have endured at least half a day of hardships showing up here. Some of them know a little English, albeit poorly. We communicate mostly with hand signs and now and again I throw in some Arabic phrases which light up everyone's faces. After thirty minutes the gates suddenly open and the mood changes radically. A small convoy drives in onto the inner court. For a moment you can't see your hand in front of your face due to the sudden dust. An obviously high-ranked figure, recognizable by the plaque of pin insignias resembling a Mondriaan painting, pinned to his chest, is furious. In a tyrannical way he shouts about, pointing at the gates basically giving instructions to kick me out asap. With hanging heads the men half drag me to where I came in earlier. Before forcibly throwing me back out into the desert they wink and smile as a way of letting me know they don't agree with this kind of policy. I'm humbled by the soldiers' gestures but I feel bad for them. All they wanted was a chance to get to know a man from another culture. They finally had the opportunity to chat with a westerner and now this is taken from them. Admittedly, they may have stepped over the line by not obeying protocol, and they may have been disobedient concerning direct orders of the officer but at the end of the day we're all people.

In an Islamic country like Jordan most hardworking citizens want to live in peace. However, interest in foreign societies, especially in the morally empty western ones, is directly penalized by the ruling organ. The West is most reprehensible to a large number of leading Muslims. They divided the world into two categories according to their holy scriptures, the *Dar es salaam* and the *Dar al harb*, meaning the house of peace and the house of war. Well, I'm not implying anything here, but you can figure out yourself which category you belong to, being a non-Muslim. Since they don't have religion and state separated, everything is ruled by their law. Sharia has the final say.

As the course advances the fight against exhaustion amplifies. Encompassed by sand there seems to be no relief. Eventually a white van pulls over, the thing nearly falling apart. A man wearing a spotless turban steps out from the vehicle and offers a cluster of grapes. Me nibbling away he asks if I needed a ride. Without hesitation I nod, I am too weak to take one more step anyway. The helpful, black bearded man has a posture too big for the small van. He's comically crammed in between the seat and steering wheel. Lo and behold, we reach a paved road about fifteen minutes later. He takes me to a red painted kiosk at the edge of a cliff, looking out over a small valley with one foot high shrubs, that are tussling plastic bags whenever a breeze sets up.

It's one of those places where truck drivers stop for a cup of coffee. Cheap plastic chairs and some tables in front of the establishment stand on a flattened strip of dirt. Luckily for me it is custom in the Arabic world to treat the stranger well, thus I am granted something to drink and a meal with rice and chicken. I'm so hungry I start stuffing my mouth straight away like an impure swine. I get short of breath because my esophagus is severely dry which is even preventing me from swallowing the road side dish. When I try to flush it down with water it is just not wet enough. Practically suffocating in my own food I realize I'm no good to maintain my desert hike, at least for now. By the time one of the truck drivers mentions I can ride along I pick my backpack from the ground and throw a smile at him, saying, "Show me the way!"

Heading towards town I dream of having a shower. I can hardly remember the last time I properly washed myself, but frankly I don't care too much because the smells from my armpits are still socially acceptable. In the banner-overlaid cabin it's very spacious and the invigorating air-conditioning knows how to turn me into a human being again. My driver wears a grey beard and a royal-blue cap on his head. He likes to listen to secular music with his son, who sits silently in the back of the cabin, shamelessly staring at me with his mouth open. During the ride I witness other drivers stepping out from their trucks. Wondering what they're up to, I see them placing a small rug on the sand only to kneel down to pray right next to the road with their engines still running! I've got to hand it to these folks, they are definitely devout. Practicing believers are obligated to repeat this five times a day. As you may well know, this is one of the five pillars of their seventh century religion, or as some like to call it, authoritarian ideology. Reaching the suburbs of the capital Amman the grit truck empties its cargo which heralds the end of Amal's long workday. Since we don't speak each other's language not many words are shared, so the outcome sometimes has been a bit awkward. My attentive nature causes me to understand him most of the time though. In this case, that means I know he'll take me to his house to have supper.

Located on a hillside, the terrace on top of this apartment building bestows a magnificent view across the valley. For as far as the eye can see there are residencies by the thousands, all jam packed and shoulder to shoulder. Basically, they're nothing more than square concrete boxes in comparable colors. The only thing sticking out, and quite literally in that sense, is a gigantic white landmark called the Raghadan Flagpole. Towering all surrounding hills, it is ridiculously tall with a height of at least four hundred and fifteen feet. Evenly impressive is the nation's flag attached to it, its dimensions being thirty meters by sixty meters. When it was erected it actually was the tallest pole in the world. It is recorded to be spotted from as far as fifteen miles away and when it is lit up at night the pole boasts a dignified allure.

Before I enter the house my driver hides his wife in the kitchen. I am not allowed to see her. How different from the West, where introducing your wife is likely the first thing you do! Over here men dominate every aspect of society. A quick introduction to his children follows, yet while the boys linger, his daughter is off to the kitchen also. Having washed our hands, we are now ready to eat a variety of traditional Jordanian snacks which are being served by his daughter on what seem to be silver platters. After the meal the old truck driver lights up a big, fat joint. It's insane how many people are using this illegal plant. Even though I do not meet anyone who doesn't smoke, I politely decline. Like most other locals, he too is completely confounded to hear that I never used cannabis in my entire life. Not even during my five years of living in Amsterdam, where it's legal to do so, but I am not claiming to have always been a saint. Other substances have been marked on the checklist. When the last cup of tea is consumed, the family suddenly says goodbye. The oldest son opens the gate and takes me to the streets. I have no idea what to expect, other than realizing that they don't want me to spend the night at their place, since they are more or less sending me on my way now.

Out of some twisted habit the unkempt boy is constantly spitting on the ground. For that reason, I'm not too sorrowful when a bus arrives. Boarding the bus, a question mark appears above me, like the flames on top of the heads of the disciples. Crazy as it seems, the passengers enjoy the same habit and spit anywhere they can. Disgusting. Receiving anything but happy looks I begin to wonder if it's something else than a habit. Perhaps I'm not welcome here and this is how they choose to show me their contempt. Either way, it appears quite disrespectful. We only have one thing in common. All of us get kicked out in less than an hour at the end of the line, next to an empty square. And just like that I'm on my own again. Now that the sun has set there's only one thing I can do really, and that's finding myself a place to crash right here in the center of Amman.

Coincidentally, the last bus stop is exactly where I wanted to go, namely the very heart of the city. The gloom of the last daylight illuminates a Roman theatre. Ecstatically situated against a hillside, this two-thousand-year old structure is the nation's largest, boasting a staggering thirty-three rows of seats going upward. In fact, it is in such a good condition, conjoined with impeccable acoustics, that performances are held there today. How about that? Beautiful tall palm trees and lights from closed shops make it less of a hostile environment.

For the lack of finding something better, the benches in a park will function as my bed tonight. It's actually not that disappointing when you keep your standards low. With the time already around midnight I'm not too worried about comfort either and it doesn't take very long before I doze off. Correspondingly, it doesn't take very long before I wake up again too, from a bright light shining in my face, a shame it isn't the redeeming morning sun. Instead two police officers almost ignite me with their flashlights. Against my will I'm taken to the station where a meager inquisition takes place. It's hard to make sense of it all but I pick up some words here and there. It becomes clear to me that the officers reckon it too dangerous for me to sleep outside alone. Especially now with the current elections going on where sudden riots break out all over the place. It is nice and encouraging to know that they are doing their best to keep a foreigner safe. I'm released with the urging advice to book a hotel in the neighborhood. Well, it's more of a demand. Of course, I don't know any hotels. Besides that, and probably more crucially, I still have no money on me. Coupled with the fact that I can barely keep my eyes open, I decide to stroll back to the park I was staying at before, where I fall asleep immediately on the exact same bench, still available. In no way am I concerned about the possibility of my backpack getting stolen, or worse.

Turns out you can't fool the Jordanian police. In less than an hour the situation repeats itself. This time the two gentlemen escort me to a nearby hotel where they order the owner to give me a room. *You see, no need to bring a travel guide along!* I cynically think to myself, somehow of the opinion that the universe will automatically balance things out. Playing by their rules I take the lift to the seventh floor.

Getting punished for my nonchalant attitude surely balances things out alright. Bed bugs are attacking from every angle, frayed curtains are saturated with smells of sweat and cigarette smoke, and in spite of it being in the middle of the night by now, the traffic outside remains loud and noisy. I shouldn't complain though. I have a private room with my own bathroom, a real soft mattress, and perhaps, yes perhaps outweighing all of this, I am out of danger from possible riots outside and get to keep my life.

Due to the itching and scratching I book myself another hotel in the subsequent days. With a safe haven on hand there's enough time to delve into this secretive culture. In the meantime I'm finally in possession of a pocket full of Dinar (the name of the currency) significantly broadening my options. A visit to the ancient ruins of the Temple of Hercules is time well spent. When seeing the enormous doorways, the myth of the demigod comes alive. He must have been huge. Besides that, the viewpoint from this hill alone is worth coming here.

Nearby parks, however, generate a nasty vibe. A surprising number of closeted gays are staring at me, way too long for my comfort. Perhaps it is some sort of secretive meeting point? Either they are smelling fresh meat, or it is just the fact that there are hardly any women in the streets. If you see a dozen of women a day it's a lot, although you wouldn't recognize your own wife. They are wrapped up from top to bottom in all-concealing black burkas.

Armed soldiers are on every street corner keeping an eye on the sporadic tumult. Due to the present elections the city is sheathed with flags and banners, posters and pamphlets. Many cars are even fully plastered with pictures of their preferred candidates, who act as political hero's over here. Not a day goes by without rallies, loud shouting or small groups fighting. It is safe to say things work a little different here, one time I even see a wheeled bulldozer with outstretched hydraulic arm, carrying three guys in its U-blade. Several times a day prayers echo from the high minarets of the King Abdullah Mosque, with its grandeur aquamarine mosaic dome. The somewhat – to some – intimidating recitation of the Qur'an are delivered by the Imams, who are masters in masquerading the indoctrinations with elegant, harmonic tunes.

Trying to convert me in the process, a portion of the few people I meet proudly show me pictures of their *Hadj*, the pilgrimage to Mecca. In spite their diligent efforts so far no one managed to do so. Having studied at a university in Jerusalem, where I was taking some classes in religion, I collected my own set of views and believes. I don't mind them trying to fulfill their task though, I understand it's part of their world and so I show respect. One that is not interested in faith is Samir, an older man from Lebanon, who owns a transportation company. Visiting Jordan for business the grey bearded man suggests we spend some time together. Guessing his intentions are good, I agree. While buying us lunch he shares considerable inside information about the state of affairs in the Middle East, yet it seems to me that he needs to get this all off his chest. I suppose it's good to ventilate sometimes. We both know that a discrete westerner is a safe place to dump valuable resources on, things better left unsaid to his direct network. He knows he is constantly being watched too. When we part ways, he realizes how much he told me thus making me swear not to tell his name to anyone. Sitting at home watching fake news on CNN all day surely doesn't teach you these life lessons, from a total stranger with half a century of experiences. Only when you decide to grab your gear and take some risk by going out by yourself, are enriching encounters guaranteed.

Time for the usual sightseeing. Let's not forget this fairly small country has much underrated richness. Undoubtedly, no one traveling here leaves without having visited the famous archaeological sites. Well, except me perhaps. Being in mid-travel flow in the north, I must confess it isn't before the last month of the year 2012 before I finally check out these next two places for myself. First, the Prediluvian Temples of Petra, that fully deserves being put on the UNESCO World Heritage list. The architecture is mesmerizing with unparalleled precision; the details and geometrical alignments still baffle engineers and archeologists today. No wonder, being designed and built with occult knowledge from descendants of the giants that still lived in those days. There's just no way the official narrative is even remotely plausible. To think that the tribe of the Nabataeans created all that with their copper chisels is utterly absurd. But hey, what do I know? Either way it is marvellous to view how the sun illuminates the red sandstone, not to mention the narrow trail with ninety-degree angled cliffs on either side, with naturally assorted complexions decorating them. You have to see it to believe it. Once it was a prosperous city due to the trade of Boswellia trees. That name probably doesn't mean anything to you, but from these they extract minerals to make frankincense, a highly valued product in those days. In the history filled air you can easily spend a day without having seen everything. I can assure you, it will leave you contemplating long after on how they were able to establish such societal superiority.

If you're so close to one of the phenomenal sensations of this earth, you can't afford to miss the Wadi Rum desert. Possibly the most genuine on this side of the heavens. Khaki dunes interspersed with deep red sand, intriguing layered rock formations abiding in primordial prudence, and an overall astounding beauty of uninhabited lands. Fortified colors are gently broken by a single viridian bush. It's not exceptional to come across camels either, dwelling abundantly on the plains. If you have a desire to feel as one with the undisturbed nature then surely this is a recommendation. Merely being here in the lonesome nothingness is a remedy for the soul, as if it were healing therapy.

Back to Amman I carry on with my voyage with my Nordic walking sticks. Cloudless skies are brighter than ever – even hurting my eyes. Intense sunshine beats down on my sunburned face. As I keep on walking my fairly new hiking boots are broken in quickly. Not keeping any track of days always produces a legitimate feeling of freedom to me. I am just a man in the world, right here, right now, and that's it. If I could only hold onto that splendid consciousness while being at work. Unfortunately, my job is too stressful to be focusing on other things. It's virtually impossible finding a balance between running a business and the much-coveted serenity. They can't coexist. Still, it's a funny thing, while working I often dream about traveling, mind you that while traveling I never dream about working.

As I flank smoldering tarmac lanes, the layer of heat rising up in the distance causes them to mirror. Then, it shows that a bus draws near from the Jett company, right through the mesmerizing mirage. As a way to cool down the engine it drives with the valve open, as all of them do. On his own initiative, the chauffeur slows down to ask if I care for a ride to the north, knowing full well that I won't survive two days here on my own. I reckon crossing a border with a group of people is easier than attempting alone, so I accept his proposal. In all of the surroundings I've met zero other westerners and inside the bus it's no different. To my relief, they at least halted the spitting.

Late in the afternoon we arrive at the border where I am interrogated for hours. So much for crossing it with a group. After a while I have to take my luggage out of the bus and remain behind. Other travelers are all granted access and sit themselves back in their seats. Closing the side hatch, they curiously peek from behind the curtains, without any sign of compassion. Returning to the Immigration office, men in suits inquire how I got into the country. If

I tell them the truth that I came via Israel they obviously won't let me into Syria, since no one is allowed to do so. This is why I travel with two Dutch passports, as I previously promised to explain. The one with stamps from Israel I mailed back to the Netherlands last week in order not to be busted. From the stamp in my second passport they assume that I can't have entered Jordan by airplane, and right they are. But I'm playing stupid and pretend I don't understand English, meanwhile trying my best to look as innocent as possible. When every attempt fails this door stays closed. What a disappointment, to get rejected so coldheartedly.

While hiking south, I'm lost in thoughts about what to do next. Dealing with the new insecurities a car pulls over with two guys inside. Generously handing over a bag of potato chips they wonder what this white tourist is doing here. Gluttonously restocking my salt level I explain the situation to them. As if sent from above they plead me to step in and accompany them to their home. No idea what to expect I give in to their persuading charms. Licking the scraps off my fingers I hop into the back. Loud, obnoxious music is blasting out of cracking speakers. Assuming that they are in their early twenties the boys are singing and clapping along enthusiastically with their favorite cassette. Pretty soon we diverge from the asphalt to a lonesome dirt road, mainly existing out of boorish gravel. Leaving a long trail of dust behind we are in for a bumpy ride. The key is pulled out of the ignition when we bob up beyond the outskirts of their hometown Mafraq.

Showing interest in one another I find out the boys are part of a family of settled nomads. It's just their house and nothing else for miles around. I'm amazed at the amount of sheep that roam about. How can they find something edible between the rocks of this barren infertility? One of their uncles, wearing a red and white checkered headscarf, is happy to see us. Within no time the whole house runs out to see me and I get introduced to the family. Other family members of surrounding villages get summoned to also behold this pale souvenir. There is this tiny voice in the back of my head questioning if my head will be severed by these barbarian people. Of course, it is totally unjustified. I'm shown great hospitality by trays of rice, chicken and various vegetables. We spend all night eating on the floor. Chairs and tables do not partake in their style of furnishing. Instead there's rugs, cushions and mattresses. When the tribal elder bestows a traditional garment I'm deeply moved. Lines in his sun darkened skin tell tales of sophistication. He just met me and already shows so much kindness. In return I give him a pair of wooden shoes with hand painted windmills on them. I often bring along portable gifts on my travels for special occasions such as this one. We both are appreciative of the gesture and enjoy mutual respect. And to receive as much as possible from my part I tried to adapt to their culture by keeping short hair, not eating pig meat and by covering my arms and legs, even in this heat. By now I learned from experience that I would have never been treated this way if I was wearing shorts or still wearing my blond ponytail. Falling asleep at night with about fifteen others in the living room, I think to myself how anyone can choose a holiday at a lowbrow all-in resort, in one of those overcrowded touristy beach towns.

Having tolerated a night of feisty snores with cliché-like odors of goat and garlic, we are on the move to a neighboring village, again leaving a long trail of dust behind us. Due to my poor understanding of Arabic, let alone their local tongues, I am completely clueless about our destination, or the reason thereof. What I *do* know is from the second we enter this small settlement, every single resident converges. Am I to expect my ritual onslaught after all? Pleased that nothing like that befalls me, we enter through a green-painted gate made from cast iron. Parking on the property of the nicest house of the street by far, with smooth plastered walls, well-maintained rose bushes, a neat pergola and a wiped-down driveway. Where am I? As it proves to be the case, they have an uncle that enjoys the rank of major in the Jordanian army. Before we enter his house he already approaches to greet us and shakes our hands. This educated individual speaks proper English, thus enabling us to have a real conversation, that he on his turn translates to his household, and the extended relatives also present for the occasion. To know that the entire tribe consists of a staggering nine hundred people! I don't think they do birthday presents over here. Anyway, small children stare without blinking, cautiously yet curiously hiding behind adult legs and all this time a large group of spectators is waiting in front of the gate outside. Perhaps hoping to catch a glimpse of me, as if I am some kind of celebrity rock star – a surreal encounter. The army commander and I talk extensively about several topics, but predictably perhaps mostly about Christianity, Islam and the Jewish-Palestinian conflict. Meeting a man like this naturally sticks for a while.

Subsequently, one of the befriended nomadic boys proudly shows me their rifles. Without firing a shot we climb back into the ramshackle car again. My personal tour guides are kind enough to drop me off at the northern border. In fact, quite close to where they picked me up the day before. Having said goodbye, it's time to put on my invisible knights' armor. Today I'm going to test my luck by pulling the same trick as a year ago, of which you could read in a previous chapter, *then* being at the front lines of India and Pakistan. In a bold yet controlled manner, fully on guard, I step into the Immigration office where I was cutthroat rejected yesterday. In the huge hangar about a thousand overbearing and impatient men are sweating profusely. Ceiling fans are too high up to have any effect at all in the heat of the day. After all, it's mid-summer. There is no such thing as queues, this concept wouldn't work in this culture where there is an evident lack of self-control, so everyone is in for their own. When it's finally my turn, I choose a window with an agent that I hadn't seen yesterday. I've always been very good with remembering faces. Evidently, I'm not the only one with that gift. Only one window next to me they change shifts. Even before finding his seat, the armed replacement looks straight into my eyes, intense enough to recognize me instantly. Of all people I can't believe I'm being confronted by the same guy from a day ago! Me being caught red handed, the man starts to shout something in Arabic while pointing directly at me! From the corner of my eyes I notice my travel documents have already received a stamp, so in a flash I slide my arm through the partly round pass-through and snatch my passport and papers, only to disappear in the swirling sea of people.

Keeping my head low, I am a needle in a human haystack. While anxiously sprinting in a zigzagging fashion, I aim for the exit where an open door co-operates in my impulsive escape.

While outside, some shrubs provide cover until the coast is clear. I don't see any surveillance cameras attached to the white facades which could give away my hiding place. Step one is indeed accomplished by officially leaving Jordan. Now I have to enter the southern border of Syria somehow with a suspicious looking passport. And just like you I'm wondering *why do I always get myself into these crazy situations?* And maybe more importantly, *how do I get myself out of them?*

9

SYRIA

Assyria, known by this name by tribes and people for thousands of years. Throughout millennia this country with solely parched lands has been victorious at times and conquered at other times. It has been inexplicably connected to war since days of old. Before the more recent war, eventually resulting in the massive European refugee crisis of which ninety percent are economic migrants and fortune seekers from other countries tagging along, we did not know much about the country. Neither was there much heard about it on the news, with the exception of the Golan Heights or an occasional car bombing or the like. Before its destruction of being utterly laid to ruins, it has to be said the Syrian Empire was captivating in many ways. I count myself lucky to be among those who've seen it in days of full glory.

Of course, just like anywhere else in the Middle East the administrative rigmarole is hideous and time consuming. Arriving at the border, after just having escaped neighboring Jordan, I am launched into a direct confrontation with red tape as I have to maneuver between three separate buildings in order to get a visa, coupons and stamps, and cash. Especially the last thing turns out a pain in the ass, because if you think you can pay the entrance fee with Syrian pounds or with Jordanian dinar you're mistaken. Necessary documents are issued only with American dollars. Aha, so you're saying the current war started when Bashar dropped the dollar? That's another story in itself. Anyway, I happen to not carry those around anymore. At a small bank nearby they refuse to exchange foreign currency which creates the next problem. To my advantage I run into a Taiwanese couple that are traveling in the opposite direction. Showing sympathy for my situation they are willing to make a monetary deal to procure some cowboy money. Once again Asians save the day. When all is settled I cross huge concrete tunnels on pillars. Above the entrance the top is decorated with a billboard size photo of the president and his father. It's hard to believe I actually made it inside the country.

Step by step resuming the journey with walking sticks in my hands, dark sunglasses on, and wearing an Indiana Jones type of hat preventing my face from burning, I find myself now on undisclosed soil. Locals are compelled to watch as I must be an attraction to their sight, and rightly so. Being the only westerner in the region and even on foot is kind of asking for attention I suppose. Intrusive as Arabs can be, I pull a crowd in no time.

From here it is one hundred and nine kilometers to Damascus. According to my calculations about a three-day walk. Energized by all the new impulses and being only twenty-seven years old, what can go wrong? With my hiking shoes becoming more comfortable by the minute having found their steady pace, a man pulls over with a tiny rusty truck. In the open back of the imported Chinese hovel are his two sons. Sitting on a pile of watermelons they seem pretty comfortable, or at least used to it. The hovel doesn't have air conditioning, nor a windshield either as a way to compensate the lack of it. While getting out from his vehicle the man mumbles some Arabic phrases and all of a sudden pulls out a huge knife! In my ignorance I can't imagine him starting some sort of a jihad right in front of his kids. So I just stand there watching his next move. Fortunately, he only uses the blade to cut slices off of his fruits before offering them to me. It's easy to misjudge a total stranger, but far from innocent he turns out to be. While sitting down in the dry grass enjoying a conversation I notice the man slipping my cellphone into his pocket with a stone face. I pretend I didn't see anything until our eating is finished. After all he's still in possession of a seven-inch blade. As soon as he tucks that away I demand my phone back. Now he's acting all oblivious of how the device ended up in his pants. My first real one-on-one encounter with an inhabitant and this is how I'm treated. When his hands keep reaching for my backpack it's time to move on. Occurrences like these are one of the reasons why I do not recommend girls to go backpacking by themselves.

Later that day a large green field contrasts its barren surroundings as I stumble upon a nursery for tomatoes, red peppers and some strange looking local vegetables, unfamiliar to me. Female laborers are wrapped up from head to toe. Studying their body types, I reckon they have to be young women. Only their eyes are visible and with those same eyes they are checking me out like an eagle scouting its prey. Needless to say I return the favor. Bearing in mind I haven't seen a square inch of female skin for quite a while now. In this male dominated culture my interest in the opposite sex is noticed by one of the owners. On approach Awod introduces himself politely with a smile. He doesn't hesitate to treat me to a guided tour through the fields. With his big nose, pockmarked face and grey beard, he is passionate about his work. During his verbal clarification of the growth process the girls and I are still checking each other out. Wondering what's beneath all those layers of fabric I'm not desperate or sexually frustrated, but as a healthy young man it's just nice to flirt about. You have to understand it's not like in liberated societies where women can freely choose what they wear.

When friends of the owners arrive it is time for a cup of tea. And here is where it gets confusing, mainly because local customs differ almost as much as from town to town. At one place leaving a full glass on the table indicates this was your last one, in other places that it didn't taste very good. It's like a classified form of communication. Shaking your glass with the drinking of tea means this was your last cup, while drinking coffee it means you'd like another one. How can anyone remember all these specific acts? Subdued to trying out new things I especially find the coffee indescribably atrocious. We all know Arabic coffee is strong but this plainly tastes like dishwashing liquid! To their credit I am not a coffee drinker at all. As a way of not offending them I participate in their little tradition, however as soon as I find a second where they're not paying attention I throw the coffee grounds between the tomato plants. Some of the men wear a traditional headscarf, one of them had a beautiful white garment almost reaching the ground, and yet another has a 7mm handgun in a brown leather holster on his belt. "This is for the stray dogs", he assures me with a big smile when he sees me looking at it. Even with all my travels and myself coming from a country of narrow-minded prejudice I'm still not used to people openly carrying arms.

In the heat of day, while still gathered in the fields together, the gentlemen pursue me to come work for them. Since the salary is far below minimum wage their offer is graciously declined. A few weeks later I end up regretting this choice for several reasons. I think I really missed out on a great experience here. I do give in to their plea however of staying for the night. A mute Arabian prepares the unvaried dish of rice and chicken. Their home-grown veggies are outstandingly tasteful. Definitely no GMOs or disease fabricating Monsanto seeds. Apart from them trying to convert me we have an interesting and openhearted dialogue about politics and personal stuff. When the end of the day draws near my hospitable hosts have a huge surprise for me.

I know they have carefully listened to my stories when the mute, after being directed, pulls a motorcycle from underneath a tarp from behind the beige yurt. There's no way this is real. It's a Jialing! The same crappy brand of my Chinese bike that I had so many adventures with in Asia. While the men get down on their little rugs facing Mecca to heed the religious calling of the five pillars, I get the opportunity to drive their motorcycle through the tomato fields! With a setting sun behind the contours of distant mountains, rapidly turning the orange heaven into pink, my heart melts from the oh so recognizable sound of the engine and the smell of gasoline fumes, of which the molecules probably still reside in my pores. It's one of those rare moments where I almost share tears of sheer happiness. Hardly ever have I felt more alive than I do now. Playfully crossing through the dirt, I realize that these may actually be the best years of my life. When it's almost too dark to drive I even go for another round on a different bike. An old corroded Satar to be precise. Who knew that the sensation of riding an iron horse gives so much *joie de vivre*. I love it!

Having spent the night outdoors between vegetables I leave within the first rays of sunshine, already admirably dynamic for this hour. Every once in a while a shepherd crosses the road with a herd of underfed sheep and a handful of goats. A bundle of yurts on the horizon reveals nomadic tribes wandering these barren lands. It's a privilege to get a taste of what their existence must be like. Shadows from sporadic shrubs on the roadside are taken advantage of by salesmen trying to pawn off fruit and nougat, stacked into wooden crates. When shrubs aren't big enough a prismatic parasol does the trick, with a folding chair beneath providing the necessary relief. You can say what you want about these bearded ramblers but pretty much everyone I meet hands out free drinks and free food, ranging from tea to juice, from figs to apples or candy.

With a sunstroke provoking climate, I turn down nothing. Still, no matter how much enters my stomach my body remains somewhat powerless. For this reason, I agree to join Mohammed, a random stranger who just invited me to his home in the next upcoming village. And he intends to defy the challenge by driving us there on his dinky moped. It's a preposterous sight, me with my backpack and walking sticks on the back, the overweight Muslim in the middle, and a huge just purchased watermelon on the front in a basket too small to carry it. You have to see it to believe it! Schlepping into the peripheries of the town of Sheikh Miskeen, I'm perplexed to find a century-old Orthodox church, not too big and not in the best possible state but still nice. Not having to walk for ten minutes I'm securely reveling with my boots skimming just above the road surface from off the little backseat. In doing so, I find the opportunity to keep my eyes peeled and soak up the local practices. Who could have known that they were shy years away from a battle that would leave no wall standing? But so far so good. Reaching Mo's home I come to the conclusion that I'm making a habit out of getting invited by owners with the nicest houses in the neighborhood. I don't know why this keeps happening to me. New window frames, snazzy wall plaster covering the exterior and in spite of serious water shortage Mo managed to create a decent garden. Before I'm allowed into the house he swiftly hides his wife in the kitchen, giving her clear instructions not to come out without his permission. I am not introduced to her nor do I ever catch a glimpse. Although this happens everywhere I go I can't get used to it. It is totally bizarre in my western mind. Mo walks back and forth to the kitchen to collect the wonderful dishes his wife is making. In the living room the platters are diligently placed on the blue pile carpet on the floor. No one seems to have a table around here. I bet the first Syrian based Ikea is yet to be build.

While getting to know each other it turns out that my new friend is the proud owner of a few acres of farmland. Understandably it's time for the two of us to get on the dinky moped again, this time without the watermelon in the front. He wishes to show me his self-made enterprise. Arriving at the scene he calls out for his workforce as he contrives coffee and tea. When everyone enters the fairly large open tent, functioning as a grubbing shack, I witness about forty eyebrows rising, and with it a look in their eyes that say *where the hell did you get this one?* Me and Mo being the only ones speaking English the situation is just a little bit uneasy, just a little.

During our absence from his house the concealed woman makes a five-star supper that I won't forget easily. I'm constantly stressing: "Thank your wife from me!", but there's no way of telling if he actually does. We mainly discuss polarities about religion, faith and politics. He even shares very personal stories he hasn't been able to tell his closest friends. Things such as the passing away of a child, not being able to make new ones, and contentions typical for a marriage. It is commonly expected here that certain things are meant to be kept to yourself. In my opinion these people are making it hard for themselves. Of all the things spoken of there's something else I won't easily forget. And that is the fact his wife will sleep alone in bed tonight in a separate room while we are on mattresses on the floor in the living room. Un-freaking-believable.

When the trip proceeds, there are times when I get offered coffee ten times a day. If I would respond to all the requests I would still be there today. At other times there is nothing but endless forsaken landscapes. Overall, it's getting harder to find shelter at night. In this militarized zone the sandy hills are fancied up by entrenched bunkers on either side of the road. Barren wastelands have a certain beauty to them. The overall vibes are gradually turning hostile but the simplicity of the bleakness is captivating. After roaming for a while in scorching heat a village appears on the horizon. A quick check proves it's too small to be mentioned on my roadmap. Moving towards my new goal I am more or less six hundred feet away when my legs become elastic, straps of my backpack are cutting in my shoulders, and hunger and thirst cause me to give in to my exhaustion. I drop to the ground and can't make one more step. The village is right there and I cannot reach it. Incredible heatwaves rob me of all my energy. Because I get completely ignored by the few cars that pass, it takes me at least two hours to gather enough strength to army crawl to the first shop, where I drown myself in ice cold revitalizing fruit juice. To regain my former level of vitality I rest for another hour in the shadow, relaxing on a plastic chair belonging to the store. Now that I am here anyway I also order a great tasting falafel sandwich and gather possible life-saving provisions for the road ahead.

Meeting a group of accommodating villagers in the vicinity they propose to take me to the next small town in their ragged BMW. Upholstery of the leather seats is torn to pieces with springs nearly sticking out. Cigarettes piled up in the ashtray spread intoxicating smells. Rusty scratches and dents on the exterior, the antenna broken off, and I'm willing to bet if you'd kick the bottom from the inside hard enough you will go straight through. Sounds great! Once there, it's literally nothing more than one unpaved thoroughfare with a few side streets. This town is so small it doesn't even have sidewalks. It goes straight from your front door into the dirt. They manage to find me a shelter for tonight in an abandoned storefront, or so I think. It starts out okay in a friendly atmosphere, in some sort of tavern we eat and drink all evening. Because of the language barrier I am mostly left alone sitting on my stool at the bar. When the hands of time herald midnight the unthinkable happens. Without mercy they kick me out onto the street! I'm just in time to gather my belongings before they lock the doors behind me. I guess someone had one drink too many, and it ain't me! Now I have to find something else in a state where I should have been in dreamland already.

As hot as the days in the Syrian desert are, nights can be treacherously cold, close to freezing point. This is one of those nights. After I shake off a pack of stray dogs I realize everyone is sleeping at this late hour in this dead-end town. Wandering to the edge I find an abandoned wooden carriage with some cucumbers that someone apparently forgot. Not knowing who they belong to I make them mine. Too bad for the flies that are already laying eggs in the skin. For about an hour I scout the inky perimeter before the cold forces me to set up camp. Unfortunately, there is no camp to set up, the only thing I have is a slim thermo mat and the same not so good fleece blanket

I've been dragging along since the beginning. A shallow hole is dug with a dead tree branch, rocks are piled up to prevent the now howling winds to penetrate, which it does anyway, even chilling the marrow in my bones. Around me are the shards of glass from smashed beer bottles, millions of stars in the black sky, dogs barking at a distance too close for comfort and I am left shivering uncontrollably all night without closing an eye. It's one of those long wrecking episodes of sleep deprivation you will always remember.

A descending layer of warm air makes me perceive it has to be morning. Stinging eyes from fatigue, parched skin, my clothes dirty and wrinkled. With a thousand perils lying in wait I'm relieved to have survived this one. Gently lifting my head, I detect three kids climbing a barbed wire fence to check if I am dead or not. All they could see from the roadside was a partly hidden lifeless body. Now that they find me breathing they are happy to give me a small melon, just like that, and then they mysteriously vanish back into the desert. Some farmers that happen to pass by look envious at my gift as I start eating right away. This, together with half a cucumber injects just enough fuel to hit the road again. So there I go with my walking sticks through the world's arena. Little did I know that today would have a giant trick up its sleeve, one of exponential proportions.

Torridness all around, as far as the eye can see nothing can quench my thirst. Only an endless prison of sand. As in previous days the sun heats up the earth rapidly. At one point when I am leaning on one of my sticks catching my breath I note a trail of dust afar. With the cloud getting longer and bigger I conclude that the object is coming my way, after assuming it's a car I resume hiking. After all I am in dire need of water and provision. When the sound of the engine reaches my ears the object, indeed a car, is heading straight towards me. With notable velocity they pass me on the left and pull the breaks mere yards in front of me. Doors open and three Arab men jump out and grab me! *Okay this isn't happening,* I think to myself. But it is. They drag me across and push me into the vehicle, with my backpack still on. In broad daylight I get kidnapped! It all happens in a split second. Before I fully grasp what's going on I am already surrounded by the sunglass-wearing individuals and we are on the move. Where will they take me? What will they do to me? Who are they? Despite these nagging questions I remain surprisingly calm. In fact, I don't think for a second about escaping or a counter attack. Jumping out of the car is not an option anyway with zero possibilities to hide on the plain. When I curiously ask what the hell this is all about, they remain silent, without turning their heads.

Once we arrive at a location we enter a small building in the middle of nowhere. As they are going through my stuff I'm seated on a chair at a desk. Except for a folder, an office lamp, and a ball point pen it is empty. In an unguarded moment I snatch the pen and quickly put it in my left pocket. In case things do turn ugly I now have a weapon to defend myself with. The things you learn from watching action movies. None of them speak proper English, but the reason for keeping me hostage becomes clear soon enough. They suspect I am an Israeli spy. Really? "A Dutch backpacker making his way through the desert on his own is suspicious to you?", I ask in an agitated manner. Repeating the question in my head I realize I'm not helping my case. After hours of interrogation they switch to suspecting me to be an American spy. All this time they haven't introduced themselves nor are they planning to do so. Trying to figure out what the deal is I do know they're not amused about the missing SD card in my digital camera. The only place where they didn't frisk me upon entering the facility is my left coast pocket, and guess where I'm hiding it? In fear of getting mugged or my camera somehow getting stolen I have the habit of separating the memory card from the device, which turns out to my luck today.

While noticeable aggravated, their hairy hands keep on searching through my luggage. Meanwhile I boast that my embassy expects me to report back to them daily, and that they are aware of my exact location. "They are probably already looking for me right now!" I try to mess with their minds to get out of this situation as fast as I can. It works. Immediately the atmosphere changes and I notice this gets under their skin. This is a strong indicator I'm most likely dealing with the Syrian Homeland Security. Actually, that is a big relief. Obviously, they don't want any trouble with this foreign national. Since they can't find the right evidence of how I crossed the border with Jordan we hop back into the car, early in the evening. Me and the three angry faces drive way out through the desert, even further as where they had plucked me from off the soil. Eventually they throw me out at a random spot never to be seen again. Hereby killing the opportunity for me to receive some kind of ration I was hoping for so badly. It seems like it will be another night with an empty stomach out in the cold. Sometimes you are in the groove, other times you are in the gutter, yet at the end of the day always prevailing because what a crazy day of traveling this was!

Not long after I stumble upon a paved road. Slowly sloping its way upward traffic signs cease to exist. My reward for all these hardships is waiting for me on the other side of the ledge. From this viewpoint the massive oval valley reveals itself, with in it the two million inhabitants of Damascus! Wiping my dust-covered face clean, I am finally here, having walked the thousands of years old route, where many have gone before.

The sound of a car horn interrupts the moment of awe and orientation. Passersby make note of the Syrian flag tied to my backpack that I found along the way. Two flabby guys in a tin can on wheels pull over to start a conversation. I guess the city itself has to muster patience a little while longer, for I have rendered to their invitation and make my way to their home. Friends back home always wonder how I end up at people's houses. Well this is how it goes: it just happens.

We exit the tin can into one of the suburbs, recognizable by the square sand-colored houses. Due to its low-rise features, it has this typical Arabic starkness. Upon inspection, by no means do the boys have their own space, as much as three whole households are stacked in the compound. All relatives though. An elderly lady observes me from head to toe before she stuffs me with food and recommends a few hours of sleep. These folks reckon that having a guest is an exceptionally serious business. Especially when it concerns a guest from another country. From the minute I arrive they are showboating the heck out of it. Decanters of delicious sweet tea, all sorts of fresh fruit, and the irretrievable dish of rice and chicken. The eldest towel-head, a sort of a chieftain, takes my dirty socks that I've been wearing for days and presses them firmly against his nose. Even before I get a chance to stop him he inhales deeply with his eyes closed. To this day I don't know if that's one of his suppressed sexual desires, or what, but the way he looks at me right after with that smirk on his face is disturbing to say the least! An additional bliss comes when he starts washing my dirty clothes with water and soap. After I take a shower, which they insisted I should get, I am hoisted in a spotless white robe. Why am I treated so courteous? For a second the crooked thought creeps up that they want me pure and fattened for the ritual slaughter awaiting me. Yet nothing can be further from the truth.

Accompanied by the sweet fragrance of a huge jasmine tree overhanging the contiguous garden, a snug inner court is where a large portion of the big family gathers. Besides begging me to stay with them for a whole week I receive a lot of questions. One member teaches English at a university, thus functioning as the interpreter in the hearing. All are interested in learning more about my stories of travels abroad, since none of them were able to leave the country. We talk for hours on end, we smile and we laugh and it's legitimately good company. It all runs smoothly until the verbal atomic bomb drops that changes everything.

They ask for my opinion about Israel. I actually risk getting kicked out of the country or at least getting arrested and jailed when I decide to trust them by stating that I just came from the Abrahamic lands. In doing so I am literally one phone call away from handcuffs and possible beating, or worse. Luckily they are struck with disbelief of my experiences and too astonished to walk away from the conversation. But it is remarkable to witness such friendly people turn into savages when it comes to this subject. Commonly known lies about killing babies and the like are utterly insane. Of course they are brainwashed from early on, I have seen the children's cartoons on television myself in this region, where they indoctrinate the little ones with horrible propaganda. Let alone what the holy Quran openly says about the Jews, which anyone can read. Although they beg me to stay for another week I sense that I need to keep on moving. Who knows? Maybe I have altered their opinion about their ancient brothers from the pastures of old after all. Coexisting with people from another background is definitely an art in itself. Another thing that doesn't necessarily keep me lingering is the absence of something as simple as toilet paper or an actual toilet for that matter. I am left to shitting in a hole in the floor. Here a flimsy tube with a meagre trickle has to do the trick. No hand soap around. While minding my business I remember how we just all ate from the same platter with our bare hands. It doesn't take very long for my bowels to become insubordinate. You gotta love backpacking!

In an era before decent smartphones I search for hotels in an internet cafe, which Damascus has no shortage of, but nothing seems to be available. Wondering about the next step on the sidewalk in the sunshine, a French bloke passes. When we make eye contact he directs his steps toward me. By using his Lonely Planet we find a hotel with the only free room in town. It is no surprise when it turns out two stars less than mentioned in the guidebook. Once checked in I can start making new plans.

I mapped out a route that leads me to Mosul in the north of Iraq. I would love to visit the biblical Nineveh to marvel at its renowned ruins and statues of the civilized empire of the Babylonians, not yet smashed to pieces by future terrorist organization ISIS, but I will never make it that far. On the very next morning when I plan to head in that direction, I watch the disappointing news at breakfast. After many months of stability in that area, new terrorist attacks have arisen, making my new desired destination a no-go area.

Now that this idea is off the table I roam the narrow streets of Damascus. They are narrow enough to have to walk around the bronze lamps and Persian carpets displayed by locals hoping to make a buck. The stores in the alleyways are perfumed with spices and grilled meat, making one go back in time instantly. At the eastern gate Bab Sharqi I stumble upon the Chapel of Ananias. You know, according to the traditions this is the disciple that is send to aid the Apostle Paul, who turned blind on the road. This is the supposed location as to where he received his eyesight back. Even the exact site of his baptism is still intact. Within walking distance from the chapel is the Souq al-Hamadiyyeh which is the largest roofed market of the country. Here you'll find anything you wish for on a cultural artistic level, including a whole bunch of sophisticated junk. At the end of the bazaar you'll end up at the citadel of the Omayyaden Mosque. Like in most places in the Middle East, this one also is built on top of a former Byzantine basilica. The last mentioned was dedicated to the head of John the Baptist, who's remains appear to be in the tomb inside. Such a melting pot of rich history, the Romans worshipped Jupiter here and the Muslims their moon god Baal. Another hotspot is reserved for the old tomb of a Kurdish general who succeeded the crusaders on the throne back in Jerusalem, better known as the warlord Saladin. Basically it is one big religious enchilada. All sorts of old tales go about – perhaps most remarkable is the one about Jesus. For when he returns, so the residents believe, he will kill a beast with one eye prior to leading into a great battle of killing all the Jews. It's laughable at best. I guess we just have to wait and see how that one plays out.

In one of the wriggling alleys a shop owner tries to ply me useless souvenirs before offering me some tea. He reckons the longer I stick around the more his chances increase. Lost in compelling dialogue about Christianity a man joins our little tea party. Big scars on his neck make me wonder about what happened to this individual. I won't have to wait very long for an answer. When he mingles in our talk it turns out he is a genuine Hezbollah fighter! As recent as last year he was involved in a battle in the south of Lebanon against Israeli soldiers. He counts himself lucky to be alive, lifting his T-shirt he shows more brutal scars all over his body. "From a grenade impact!" he says, almost in a proud way showing his teeth. For me personally an incredible opportunity, less than two months ago I talked with the Israeli Defense Force on my way to occupied territory, now hearing both sides of the story. A privilege neither parties have. If I would have been honest to the authorities about my passport, the chance would have been taken from me as well. Having shook hands with both interested parties the bitter realization sinks in that in different circumstances these men would have gotten along with each other just fine. We live in a crazy world.

After a visit to a movie theatre where everyone jumps up with their right hand placed over their heart when the national anthem plays through the speakers and the flag is shown on the screen, the journey marches on. Quite literally in this particular case. Armed with Nordic walking sticks and good spirits several hard dirt roads lead north. Admirers provide me with free dates and fresh berry juice. Arbitrary goat herders arrange destitute places to crash for the night and teach me how to count to ten in Arabic. Out of politeness I pretend to like their vomit stimulating coffee, luckily the light the bonfire produces is too weak for them to notice me tossing it away. At one of the lonely crossroads a blue traffic sign with a white arrow points right reading 'Bagdad'. Having overcome the temptation to diverge I keep on going. Deeper into an area that becomes too harsh even for shepherds and nomads. Being close to the main road, redemption is neigh. Three soldiers in a taxi pull over when they spot me traversing ankle deep sand. Their generosity takes me all the way to the forthcoming place, the city of Homs. Today nothing more than a flattened-out blueprint of concrete rubble and warped steel. Years of warfare have unfortunately made it utterly unrecognizable. When I arrive it's a prosperous town with hardworking people. It is interesting to me that faces from the local population have drastically changed, Turkish influence is undeniable. With a current from south to north the Orontes river defies the natural laws, if I may speak in terms of scientism. At the reception desk of a cheap hotel the clerk is surprised I pay in Syrian pounds. They are used to tourists, at least the few ones taking the time to stop by, paying in US dollars.

If you are thinking about spending the summer holidays here do not expect to find streets of vibrant nightlife, where you can get drunk or walk around shirtless without getting harassed. Even in these boiling temperatures all parts of skin are covered. A lot of them even far exceed my own short temperedness, and they just have a different set of believes about liberty. For instance, if you vote for another candidate than the ruling establishment, a group of men will show up on your doorstep, using violence when required. Knowing this, it seems less of a miracle getting the same President elected every time, for it is solely out of fear.

When sightseeing continues a fairly big roofed market nearby is imposing as well as entrancing. Of course the main attraction is the two-thousand-year-old Orthodox Cathedral of Holy Mary, the Om al-Zenar in Arabic. Distinctive from the Catholic church and underground Evangelical ones, this one houses seven holy relics, making it a center of pilgrimage. Most famous of all is the belt of Mary given to St. Thomas as a sign. Allegedly he's the only one that saw her being carried off to heaven by angels. This remarkable conclusion was made after cross referencing some forgotten scrolls, found during renovation work beneath the altar in 1852. When I find the cathedral in a dodgy neighborhood it is actually closed, but sent from above is a sacristan who was willing to show me around. On the square outside in front of the place of worship I meet a guy my age. Malik has a lot of insider information about the situation in his country and the circumstances Christians truly face. To the outside world it is portrait that everyone with a different background lives side by side, according to mainstream media it is even as peaceful as ever. However, of the daily oppressions is never spoken. Biased jurisdiction will only allow certain things, but don't mistake that for freedom. I won't bore you with all he has to say, still, to me it is of great value. My journalistic heart writes everything down. We spend time sharing knowledge until it's close to dusk and I have to be getting back. Better go now while it's still safe for a prominently present white guy like me.

In aiming towards the next large city I come across Aleppo. If you are keen to follow world news, this name might ring a bell. Due to its industrial nature it has a different atmosphere. When I enter it's nothing less than the hustle and bustle of city life. People are running to and fro. Unlike today when streets are empty, except for the amount of debris of buildings that got the shit bombed out of them. Aleppo's eponymous castle is the predominant point of interest. Encircled by a dry canal of thirty yards wide and twenty yards deep, the indestructible fortress stands on a superficial hill towering above town. Light rocks transform almost insidiously into building blocks of the settlement supposedly in existence since the beginning of times. Separate tribes conquering the sand hill created different styles, and earthquakes had a way of altering the layout now and again, now in present form about as old as Amsterdam. With three steel entrance doors in a gate, an amphitheater, watering holes exceeding a depth of three hundred feet, and spotlights shining upward outlining the thing when dark, it is worthy to be called a *pièce de résistance* of craftsmanship. Essentially there's hardly a limit to the things I discover, not to mention the indisputable miracles that occur, but those metaphysical confrontations are for another time. For now, it means I am bound to leave these dry, outstretched lands behind.

The decision has been made to move up north towards new adventures and towards the border that looks forward to receive me.

Still I will never forget how special it is, me being one of the last people getting the opportunity to experience the country as it truly was, flourishing as in centuries of old, and alas before it got totally shredded and ripped to pieces. What a sad story. RIP Syria. May you revive again!

10

KURDISTAN

Simple things in life can truly be a consolation. For example, witnessing dry lands transform gradually into fruitful landscapes with patches of green, I feel hopelessness finally fading away. Ever since this journey on foot began at the old city gates of Jerusalem, now months ago, it was bleak and parched up to every horizon. Each new day presented a battle against the scorching heat. The windows are slightly rolled down of a car belonging to a random guy I paid off, who was willing to drive the last ten miles to the border, presumably because he had nothing better to do anyway. As I pass a huge, seemingly infinite queue of stationary semi-trucks, salt air reveals the close proximity of the romantic Mediterranean Sea, causing excitement to be perceived by my underbelly. A basic building with big red flags with a white star and crescent moon sticking out heralds the mediocre guarded frontier line. One never knows what to expect at this type of crossings, meaning over land, but everything runs flawless for a change. With a new visa in my passport, I safely make it into the most southern part of central Turkey.

While mass tourism is solely clumped in the western provinces, focusing on that side of the country alone, this area managed to preserve its authentic character. Here where the undiscriminating slow current of the Orontes river flows further inland the riches of Antakya are protected by the magnificent Amanus Range, nowadays known as the Nur Mountains. Rustic dark brown peaks aren't the only things that changed their name, for the city itself was formerly known as the biblical Antioch. According to legend it's on this latitude where the followers of Jesus were first named Christians. Shrouded in antiquity the remains of huge walls from later times in history tell tales of the important role it played during the defensive campaign of the Crusades. What a time that must have been, when the brave knights of Europe were fighting for what they believed in, in order to save their Judeo-Christian heritage.

With renewed vigor I begin to hike eastward. As my directive I use the position of the summer sun, but not for long. That same sun in combination with weeks of malnourishment and dehydration makes me feel weak and fatigued. The endless lanes of cracked asphalt are pursued with a clearly decreasing pace until I reach a mental juncture.

Why am I inflicting this self-mortification to my own body? Infrequent passing tour busses beckon me to join. After some inner resistance I give in at one point. For a handful of lira you can buy a bus ticket for a ride that lasts forever, so who am I kidding really? Once on board I slump down in my chair almost convinced I deserve this. For some unjustified reason I feel a bit guilty anyway – forsaking my reliable walking sticks like this. I check out my fellow passengers: some are wearing headscarves, males and females alike, some are wearing sweatpants with tuxedo shoes while others have an old revolver tucked in their leather waistband. Not really knowing what to make of the last thing I definitely don't feel unsafe. Yet at the same time I reserve a part of my consciousness to stay vigilant at all times.

In the many hours that follow we pass through mountains and sloping valleys. One can't help noticing the increasing number of roadblocks and check points. This continues until we penetrate deep into borderless Kurdistan, reaching the timeworn city of Van in the Far East, not too far from the Iranian border. Still four years away from a devastating earthquake that would absolutely flatten the place resulting in hundreds of deaths and thirteen hundred wounded. In Central America I have been exposed to the sudden dangers of true earthquakes a number of times, but so far always made it out alive and without any harm done.

As peaceful as it seems now, the centuries of violence and conquering nations left traces of epic wars. From the Armenians to the Byzantines, from the Mongols to the Ottomans and lesser known conquests. Most intriguing is the brick fort built right outside the city. It is situated on a high rock built by the first documented inhabitants of the kingdom of Urartu, one of earth's most ancient tribes. Besides the strategic location it also has a breathtaking view on the lake and hilly surroundings. My mind goes slightly hysterical when I discover carved inscriptions of Xerxes the Great on the rocky wall of the citadel. This king of Persia is interpreted in the Book of Esther as Ahasuerus, most likely the father of Darius the Mede. If only a time machine existed you could witness the magnitude of the military undertakings that became a way of life for many. Standing here with closed eyes taking in deep breaths of air I sense the endless caravans leaving their tracks in the sand; the horses, the carriages, the camels, the soldiers, the slaves, the Silk Route comes to life. Clinking sounds of swords, harnesses, and all sorts of steel, as well as the trampling of hooves. Smells of the cattle and fresh spices, and the presence of all the spoils of war from the various battles along the way. Adding to the magic is the fact that I am all by myself in these remote fields. Somehow I did it again, in the middle of high season, I am privileged to be the only Westerner close to a city of four hundred thousand heads.

With thirty degrees Celsius outside there is an abundance of good food like one can only find in the Far East. Blocks are marked by rows of comely engineering, or rather the absence of it. Since I never make reservations for a place to stay I keep my eyes open for something that feels good. While traveling a lot of these things go by intuition. Not that I always choose wisely as would soon prove to be the case. A simple three-story hotel has exactly one room available. When the bellboy, an unshaven man in his forties, carries my luggage up the stairs for lacking an elevator, he snares with a thick accent, "I hate English, I hate America and I hate Israel!" We haven't even shared words when he begins to spew his hatred. Shaking my head I wonder where this is coming from. And more importantly, *where will it lead to?*

As soon as the very next day it becomes apparent this wasn't an isolated incident. Random strangers are fishing for information, and I can't leave a single store before I answer the two unavoidable questions: "Where are you from?" and "What is your occupation?" It becomes more bizarre when I realize that even the people who don't speak a word of English, do know these two questions. Even the small children. As if they can smear stripes of war paint beneath their eyes and hit the jungle drums with any suspicious answer. Indwellers speaking a bit more English enquire what the hell a white guy like me is here for. It seems they have a hard time coping with the truthful narrative. Being a sitting duck it doesn't take very long for the police to be informed either.

In fact, during my second night in the city three police officers break into my hotel room by forcing in the door for an abusive cross-examination! Although my heart skips a beat I manage to stay surprisingly cool. They're a bit off guard by me, only wearing a towel around my waist since I just had a shower. That turns out beneficial for me as I see a chance to quickly cover my right arm that they don't pay attention to. Namely this one has a tattoo with Hebrew writings on it. If they would detect the black ink characters, allowing them to irrationally profile me, that would surely mean my death sentence. However, they do check my passport thoroughly and my backpack goes inside out. After a while they seem to lose interest due to their poor knowledge of the English language. With echoes in the hallway and with one of them walking down the stairs I get the strange feeling the entire city knows that I'm staying here, more or less making me an easy target. Let me tell you that something like that doesn't make you particularly feel safe.

In days to come the questioning in the streets continue up to dozens of times a day. They are willing to accept that I am from the Netherlands, but me being a carpenter is unacceptable to them. At one point I get so annoyed by the ongoing persecution that I decide to play along with their little game. Call it genius or call it plain stupid but I tell a few people that I'm an arms dealer in the vicinity to trade weapons with Hezbollah. Believe it or not but from the second I do this not a single person asks me anything anymore for the rest of my whole time being here. How about that?

To keep a low profile, I visit the fort at the edge of town almost on a daily basis. The serenity is ideal to update my diary. Rustle in the dry grass makes me look up and to my surprise I see children approaching in worn-out clothes. Apparently, I'm igniting the fire with my presence. The golf ball size stones they throw at me are missing my head at mere inches! Instinctively I'm activated into self-defense mode. Quickly gathering a handful of stones myself I start throwing back, launching a counter-attack. Perhaps not the wisest decision but hey, what can you do, right? Provocatively they run past me trying to snatch my belongings. Overlooking parents are of course nowhere to be found.

Seemingly in need of goods I return the next day with a bag full of coloring books, pencil leads, and a great mood. Like lined up meerkats gazing across the savanna they notice me from afar. This time not attacking when cautiously closing in. Rascal eyes are fixated on the bag, almost bursting from curiosity and impatience. When I start handing out the gifts they yank it straight out of my hands. Even fighting each other over it, ripping the bag apart in the process. Greedy and ungrateful attitudes leave me contemplating. It is rather unsettling to see these uncontrolled critters filled with so much jealousy, this reaches far beyond random poverty. But then again, you just know that they were taught this behavior by example.

A small girl gets nearly trampled by the group before they run off to their huts and living spaces. Crouching down to her eye level I stare into black irises that don't blink a single time. Mirroring the soul, I cannot begin to imagine what those little irises have seen. No words leave her mouth, but an intense and empty glare screams from the inside out, to take her away from that place never to return. I sympathetically pat her on the head as I get up to head towards the way I came from. Fifty steps down the trail I turn around to check if I'm still safe. To my surprise the girl is still standing there in the middle of the yellow dirt road. Presumably wondering why I leave her behind like everyone else seems to do. Quickly I walk back and kneel in front of her, meanwhile scouting the perimeter in fear of retaliation of what I'm about to do. When granted a moment all alone in the universe I hold her in my arms and give her the most loving hug I possibly ever gave another human being. Overwhelmed by emotions she tries hard to receive it by absorbing a part of that energy. Slowly but steady her thin hands find the courage and comfort to squeeze back. How I would love to relieve this child from the agony and rescue her from the bitter situation she's in. Saying goodbye for the second time she knows she's the big winner of the day. No coloring book or pencil lead can match up to what she has been given. I kiss her on the forehead and my heart just breaks for leaving her behind in a world where she knows nothing but rejection. Learning to let go becomes a necessity when backpacking. No matter how dearly we desire to save the world we sometimes just can't.

Van City is not a very beautiful one. For instance, it can't be praised for things like sophisticated architecture, well-maintained parks or progressive businesses and startups. However, what it does have is a store that sells motorcycles. Seeing it by chance I can't contain my lust for adventure. Being a realist in nature I know my finances won't allow me to purchase one, but still, it won't hurt having a peek inside. Walking in the smells of brand-new rubber and iron almost put me into a trance. Four guys in their early twenties are hanging around the shop, surprised to see white skin in this part of the world. They all owning motorcycles themselves it's easy for us to connect. Before I know it I find myself on one of their rides having won their trust. Cruising streets up till the outskirts and beyond they reckon it their task to show this stranger around. Unintentionally I obtained free tour guides!

In the course of weeks we become inseparable. Every free moment the boys have they take me out to eat baklava, the super sweet Middle Eastern delicacy that makes your gums turn pale, or to have some soup and fresh fish in local restaurants, where you can spend without limit and still have money in your wallet at the end of the night. Another interest we equally share is checking out pretty girls at the romantically lit up promenade in the harbor at night. For the first time in months I see women with their hair hanging out again, as no one here cares about the hijab. And that is an interesting fact since a large majority of the population is Muslim, together with a small percentage of Yazidis, and the remaining few are Christian. As the proverbial cherry on the pie we also visit one of their more distinguished bathhouses where we have extended conversations in steam-filled quarters. I'm certainly not used to being butt-naked with other men for longer periods of time, or less long periods of time for that matter, but it definitely is an experience. Something else in the section of local unusualness is that men, as in guy friends, kiss each other on the cheeks. Doing this as a way of greeting one another is still manageable, and I actually quite enjoy the amicable gesture on account of learning customs of distant cultures, but the holding of hands while strolling the streets, oh my goodness! No offense, but how can any straight man get used to walking hand in hand with another man as if nothing is wrong? Yet here everyone does it. Essentially the act itself displays a childlike innocence and is in fact quite charming.

On one of the following days we drive through the East Anatolia province. All the way up to the shorelines of the lake being close to the Island of Akhtamar. For a nickel and dime we take the ferry, frequently going back and forth, to visit the mystical enclave. Situated at an altitude of almost two kilometers, the island's only inhabitants in sight are tortoises and seagulls. From off the rocky cliffs, about eighty yards high, the view is nothing less than breathtaking. In spite of the haziness, colors are bright as ever. Khaki mountains in the distance are mingling with the nearer darker ones as well as the endless pink flowers on the island itself. Evidently, the main attraction is the Holy Cross Cathedral, a fascinating piece of century-old Armenian heritage. Engravings on the exterior walls showcase biblical tales intertwined with folklore producing controversial giants and dragons. Understandably causing much debate among scholars. Another thing much debated, and swept under the rug on a, for lack of a better word, global scale, are the surplus of bullet holes. Sadly enough, the violence against the Armenians, leading up to the genocide with an estimated million and a half civilians systematically put to death, is still not recognized by Turkish sovereignty today. If that wasn't enough I press a wrong button on my digital SLR camera for some unknown reason, accidentally erasing most of my pictures from Syria. To anyone who has had this happening to him or to her you know how devastating that can be.

By the time I start receiving compliments that I would make a good Muslim I figure it is about time to move along. To secure a revenue I had the intention to teach English at a downtown high school, yet after a few times in front of the class I find I do not quite relate to one of the other teachers, making the decision to leave easy. In a way that is disappointing because bizarrely enough I became a respected member of society here. Some shop owners actually bought a Turkish-English dictionary only to communicate with me. How lovely is that? Such a one hundred and eighty degree turn compared to the paranoia when I first arrived. I never imagined that a moderate version of Islam could exist. Instead, people here refuse to speak and learn Arabic, abolished merely a hundred years ago as the official language, and a thing required by conservative and fundamental believers alike. Still, keeping in mind most locals still think I am a notorious arms dealer maybe I should hit the road again.

After I board the bus at the bus station, my Kurdish biker friends simultaneously wave farewell. Prior to this, we exchanged handwritten notes with our contact information. When I leave a place I always wonder if I will ever return. How easy is it to dwell on the memories of people that you shared wonderful moments with? I wonder if we will ever see each other again. Because the more you travel, the more people you get to know, and you simply can't stay friends with hundreds of people at the same time. In any case it is important to me to leave a good impression behind. Especially when you can achieve this by staying close to yourself. It is a remarkable thing to consciously grow as a person.

The wavy scenery shows off deserted farms which are the only things breaking the dry sands, even a small patch of fertile ground is nowhere to be found. Hills gradually turn into medium-size mountains. Heat of the sun increases by the minute, its brightness making me pinch my eyes. When sweat starts making its way down my back it seems the concept of wind is not invented yet. Wheels of the bus rolling along, this area is teeming with concrete roadblocks, check posts, sandbags, camouflage nets and barbed wire. Heavily armed police forces and the military alike find it necessary to storm the bus pretty much every fifteen minutes or so. Every passenger has to exit the bus to empty their bags, followed by a severe time-consuming screening. Little did I know we had just entered a zone on the brink of war: in fact, just weeks away from Turkey deciding to invade northern Iraq by an incursion, blasting the area to shreds hoping to push back the PKK. No wonder the authorities are edgy.

Having endured much hostile craziness as the only Westerner in the vicinity we finally reach a large iron gate that seems to appear out of nowhere. In big dunes behind the green-painted gate, I detect a huge billboard with a projection of spiritual leader Ayatollah Khomeini. The summer months of the year have by now turned into high season, and I suddenly realize that while my friends and former colleagues are probably standing in a traffic jam right now on some French highway, which is pretty common for Europeans in the summer I suppose, I stand here at Customs on the border of Iran! I am very anxious to see all the hidden treasures the vast plains of this country holds. The passport check takes place in an office that is partially outside and unshielded. Out of nowhere a very dark cloud appears in the clear blue sky. Up until now, I do not think I have ever seen a single cloud forming like that. Before it entirely disappears, the cloud throws down an insane lightning bolt crashing into the asphalt, just yards away, accompanied by one enormous deafening thunder. We are about twenty-five people in total and every fearful soul ducks away for protection. Even now many years later describing this I do not know the exact meaning of this wondrous event, but I do know it speaks as a predicament over me since I get coldheartedly refused. Trying to get to terms is utterly useless with these armed uniformed folks. I even lower myself to begging but it does not win them over, this time it seems I am really screwed. One meter away from prehistoric lands it becomes evident I won't set foot there. With no plan B, I feel blindsided and restless. Due to my partly Calvinistic upbringing, I cannot escape the idea sometimes that everything has to have a purpose. Many things come to mind before I accept a radical resolution has to be made.

Lost in thoughts I begin to walk back to the city of Van. A short time after, a coach slows down beside me full of illegal goods from Persia, as I find out later. When the driver asks where I need to go, I answer somewhat nonchalant while pointing towards Iran: "Anywhere but there!" Five other strangers and I climb on board to sit ourselves between stacks of packs of sodas, packs of chocolate bars and a multitude of other food products. This journey has officially come to an end. With certain pain in my heart I leave the contingency behind. Onset dusk and the bobbing of the road make my eyelids heavier than ever before until I dare to close them completely, surrendering to the comfort of not having to walk anymore. This time I won't be visiting Göbekli Tepe, presumed to be one of the oldest archeological sites known to men, nor the sites of the Seven Churches as mentioned in the Book of Revelation, as I did a few years ago.

With a rumbling stomach and a sweat-drenched long-sleeve, I finally step off the smelly bus. A very deep sigh exits my relieved lungs. Twenty-seven hours in that deteriorating chair was quite the challenge, merely surviving on chocolate bars and an occasional catnap. When the driver opens the dust-coated side hatches, he leans against them as if the hydraulic springs are too lazy themselves to do the job. After a small inspection amidst the rubble, I find my backpack before I let it rest on my aching shoulders again. By now it has morphed into the shape of my back. Incessant prayers from multiple tall slim minarets fill the old hilly city of occupied Constantinople, better known as Istanbul.

High bridges are packed with consecutive rows of fishermen. Due to reflecting sunlight the blue water glimmers like thousands of stars across the surface. Shoe-shiners with their copper instruments monopolize every street corner, keeping an eye on all passing footwear. I receive some distasteful looks when they detect my flip-flops – it's just one tourist less to scam. Accompanied by a dainty aristocratic fountain and encompassed by green lawns with bright flowers lies another eye catcher, the Hagia Sophia. This former cathedral later turned into a mosque, now being a museum under the protection of UNESCO. Inscriptions on a nearby obelisk keep me intrigued for half an hour, for whenever you see an obelisk outside of

Egypt, it is placed there with a very specific reason. Being back in the profusion of city life after months of natural solitary confinement gives me an *in your face* kinda feeling, but change is good they say. Another colorful attraction is the Grand Bazaar, a large covered market place where you can find anything you can imagine ranging from hardware to rugs, toys and souvenirs, and from clothing to spices. Here you can exercise your bargaining skills. About every ten feet, salesmen and customers are fighting real price battles. Most amusing to watch. It takes courage and experience but the more shameless you are the more profitable it gets.

Going around town in a minivan, I connect with some Turkish fellows who invite me to spend the night at their house. Because I am exhausted, I actually would have preferred to go to a hotel instead. For those of you who know me by now you'll understand I end up at their apartment anyway. Sometimes my unquenchable curiosity costs money, at other times it saves money. In the evening, we are all eating rice with our hands from the same large platter. By now, I am used to living rooms without furniture so once again I have to sit on the floor. After supper, they take their razor-sharp sabers off the wall to swing them about and play with them, even pretending to cut me in the neck to chop my head off. I don't really know what to make of it.

In the splendor of the morning I am not the only one getting up early. Streets are already filled with people. Using public transport, I am on my way to the international airport. Only three days away from my promise to give a phone call to the all-American girl I met last year in Nepal. Semi frequent email traffic has Maggie, who lives in Saint Louis, thinking I am still in some deserted desert. In a crazy turn of events I decided to not give her a call after all, but actually show up at her doorstep as a surprise! With the little financial resources I still have, I purchase a flight ticket to the New World. So long Asia Minor. Cruising above the Atlantic Ocean at a six miles height, I slowly doze away. Occasionally, the turbulence has other passengers look at my startled face. When awake I am white as a sheet, for I am at least twenty percent more afraid of flying as the maximum authorized quantity.

About ten petrifying hours later we touchdown at the O'Hare airport of Chicago. Here awaits anything except a warm welcome. After being picked out of the line a heavy interrogation follows in a small room at the militarized Immigration office where everyone is exceptionally rude. It seems that they are freaked out by my multiple visas of Islamic countries. They turn my whole life inside out while noting every detail down in a notebook. Even threatening to call up the girl I'm about to surprise – almost ruining the whole thing! Meanwhile big broad-jawed security guards nervously walk back and forth, armed up to the bone with automatic machine-guns. Many uncomfortable hours pass before this enemy of the state finally gets a stamp in his passport.

Once released into the land of the free and home of the brave, I incoherently stroll through scenes of Gotham city, with its many famous ornate bridges, recognizable from the many movies shot here. Because airplane meals do not provide sufficient nutrition, I get a meal at a Panda wok, which is a Chinese stir-fry restaurant. If I ever had a culture-shock, I have one now. On account of the season, there are girls in hot-pants everywhere, leaving nothing to the imagination, women in bikinis with long uncovered hair, and shirtless runners going about as if it was normal. Perhaps it is not completely unjustified that men from certain far-away regions view the West as immoral. There is so much exposed skin, I can hardly believe my eyes. And where are all these women coming from anyway? I can wear what I want, leaving my tattoos uncovered, and I can even say what I want, without any fear of ending up behind bars, or worse. And that is a liberty to cherish. It is beyond me, the differences between everyday life here and in the Middle East are major, and takes serious time of getting used to.

Since there is a wide interconnection of silver metros above the roads, with spray painted catchphrases on its sides, I hop on one of those for a quick visit to the Sears Tower. Nowadays under another name it will always be that skyscraper with the iconic antennas, with over five hundred meters in height, poking holes in the ozone layer. In a specially designed elevator, you're launched to the top in but nine seconds. Here one can marvel at the spectacular view from the hundred and third floor. Fading horizons in the far distance are at least as captivating as the other grey-colored high-rise down below. For those not afraid of heights they constructed glass cubicles on the exterior of the building, creating the illusion as if you are soaring in the sky. It was definitely worth the few dollars to go up there.

On later trips to the northern parts of the Americas, I often pause in this city for a few days. Its mixture of vibrant and antique styles has made it one of my favorites. To be fair it is a little bit too liberal-minded for my taste nowadays, and there is a lot of criminal activity which is an absolute shame due to so many things it has to offer. From theatre and talented musicians downtown to the engaging architecture of buildings like the train station, continuing to great parks and the shores of Lake Michigan and so much more. During my stay this particular time the agenda is unexpectedly filled with a lot of interestingness, but for now, I will highlight one funny event, so this chapter can come to a closing.

A few blocks away a small crowd gathers in front of a sizable window. With my curiosity aroused, I worm my way to the front until my nose nearly presses against the glass. Three reporters in suits are sitting behind a colored desk with bright neon lights. In front of them an entire camera crew are in action with all the fusses about them. When I ask bystanders what is happening it appears some popular sports network is on-air. Citizens come to watch the weekly sports scores being filmed and broadcasted live from this location. Both sides of the studio hosts huge screens where we as spectators outside can directly follow everything. All of a sudden the cameras turn around to point directly at the street audience with me standing at the front, meaning I am full in the picture. There you have it, not even half a day in the United States and already on national television! Everyone chants and screams in excitement for the entire world to see. Except for me, standing there I cannot help thinking, *shit I hope she's not watching right now!* Ironically almost blowing my own cover.

Walking past neat apartment complexes in residential areas, I feel the heat from the day gets more intense by the minute. Right above my head the summer sun throws down pressing rays. In addition, the weight from water bottles recently added to my luggage is starting to take its toll. In the middle of the day I am increasingly getting tired, even extremely tired. Due to the time difference it's already night at the place I just came from, over in Turkey. Not yet forsaken by the angels, destiny finds me a spot to crash in the late Sunday afternoon, right next to the lake. Because the days of John Gotti are long gone, I feel comfortable enough to stay outside. Even though they are easily as big as rats with evenly sharp teeth I pay little attention to the excess of squirrels in the patches of grass around. Sliding my backpack, still screened by a layer of dust from the Middle East, beneath a picket bench I can finally close my heavy eyes. Babbling billows lull me into a deep sleep soon after.

By the time it is pitch black I am swiftly woken by an incredibly bright light. So bright that it makes it impossible to open my eyes. When I am finally able to spawn a slight squint, I recognize the black uniforms with golden insignias instantly. Two police officers are shining their flashlights right in my face, holding the things as if they're ready to club me down any moment now. Where did I experience this before? Whilst questioning me, they lead me to the police car where I am put into the backseat. Just great. Who else manages to end up in a police car on the first day of being in another country? Little did I know; the madness had just begun.

AFTERWORD

So that was it for now. How to properly end a string of tales anyway? To know the last page of these writings is certainly not the end of the story. One might argue if a story ever truly ends in the first place. If only people keep reading and talking about it, it may actually live forever. Stories are created by dreamers, and daring to dream involves risk. Start your own search for true happiness and begin today.

Throw your television set out of the window in order to put a halt to the lies and indoctrination. Set yourself free from the utter nonsense that kills brain cells and leaves you bitter and spiritually poor. Go easy on eating pork because it's ruining your body and infects your soul, and while you're at it, try to hold back on the E-numbers as well. It might be a major change. You don't have to be a tree-hugging loony to take care of yourself. Don't be afraid of rejection or kicking useless friends out of your life who aren't real ones to begin with. What do you have to lose? Nothing. What can you gain? Precious time to invest in yourself and things that matter. If done in a natural way, working out in the gym will actually make you a better person. And for the love of God, make up your own ideas instead of letting others decide for you. Sitting home depressed, watching your life go by, or going to waste, is a destructive suicidal thing that drags you down into depths rather avoided. People who had a long and fruitful life hardly regret the things they did, yet they do regret the things they didn't do.

Being born into a family that never believed in me, where enthusiasm was mocked, creativity ridiculed and fantasy scoffed at, it was a long and heavy journey to break free from all that negative energy, for the lack of a better term.

When I was about ten years old I hitchhiked for the first time. That day I drifted from home quite a bit as a narrow trail led me to stroll along dense reed shorelines of a big lake. As usual, my eyes were set to find bird skulls and real treasures, so much so this particular time that I didn't notice massive thunderclouds rolling in. When lightning began I realized there was nowhere to hide in the unprotected open fields. At a nearby highway I put my little unsuspecting thumb up in the hope to escape the armageddon upon me. Moments before the weather would turn savage a couple pulled over in the smallest car you've ever seen. I will never forget it, behind the wheel sat a man with a long dark ponytail, silver rings in both ears, a black leather vest and his arms tattooed. Next to him an old lady with long grey hair, looking like a stereotypical witch. It took a few seconds for my curiosity to prevail over the hesitation. Seldom did I meet such lovely people though, a bit weird perhaps, but lovely. Once home, my parents were clearly more angry I got into a stranger's car than relieved I was back safely. Not a sign of concern nor compassion. It's because of this reaction I don't hitchhike even a single time in the following fifteen years.

Every once in a while you find a real home in unsuspected corners. For example, back in the early fall of 2003 I happened to be in the Swiss country side on the border with France. Leaving wooden mini villages behind I am getting ready to climb a certain mountain at the foot of the Alps. It seems a well-considered thought to ask to fill up my water bottles at a small farmhouse next to a green field with fenced-in horses. When she notices my stuttering as I try to find the right words in French, the lady of the well-maintained house shifts to German, a language we both happen to speak quite decently, when required. Chatting away about my planned solo ascension and the reason why I am dressed in a camouflaged army uniform (for me and my friends loved to have survival weekends in the woods) it turns out her daughter had communion that very morning. It is Sunday and the whole family just came back from church. Now seated at a long table with spotless white sheets, cutlery of real silver and a surplus of traditional local dishes. Although feeling a bit awkward and out of place I accept her spontaneous invitation to the celebration. Shy children observe the intruder from across the table until the first one approaches. It doesn't take very long to be surrounded by them, all wanting to take a picture with me.

One delicious lunch later the lady of the house starts off a serious conversation, leading up to her asking me about my dreams. By now it's just the two of us in a different part of the beautiful spacious overgrown garden. Unknowingly being three years away from the actual event, I open up and share I am going to Tibet to climb Mount Everest. This is on my agenda and nothing can make me deviate from this goal. Completely contrary to the patronizing responses I'm used to, she says the following that I will carry in my heart for the rest of my life: "Send me a message when you're there", meanwhile writing her contact information on a piece of paper. Wait, what? From the undeniable determination in her voice I know instantly she has put all her faith in me. Almost choking up, I detect not even the slightest glimmer of cynicism. She recognized the passion in my eyes. Perhaps for the first time in my life I feel as if someone really believes in me and my capabilities. Bizarre to get such encouragement from a total stranger.

Speaking about reaching goals, a prominent recent one is aiming to inspire others with my story. Hopefully you enjoyed reading my comprised endeavors, and join me in continuing where I left off in the next upcoming volume!

Always forging plans for future travels there is plenty to research or dream about. But first things first, every journey starts with finding the means to be independent. Some travelers choose to solely rely on hospitality of locals, disrespectfully draining them in the process. In my proverbial book there is no escaping of having to work and save. And actually, I kind of like it like that. Funding yourself gives no greater satisfaction when spending it on new experiences in far-away cultures. Already making preparations for the next incredible journey I can't wait to do what I do best. I think deep down inside I will always be that little child, sitting in the seat on the back of my mother's bicycle, ready to escape to explore the world.

To be continued...

THANK YOU

Dear Reader

Having written *Breaking Free* means a lot to me, and I feel grateful for the many positive comments I have received so far. I would greatly appreciate it if you could possibly post a short review.

Thanks a lot in advance!
Jeffrey

I will soon be releasing part 2
in the series Good To Go:
Beyond the Equator.

ABOUT THE AUTHOR

So far Jeffrey Vonk has travelled over 60 countries, and authored three books, two of which from the series of *Good to Go!*

Coming from a Dutch working-class family, he started out as a carpenter, got himself certified as an outdoor sports instructor and made it to university through pure determination.

Although Jeffrey loves being at home writing, realizing his dreams of tasting new cultures is what he does best. Ever-yearning for raw adventure, the icy trails of Mount Everest are not unknown to him, as well as meeting up with members of Hezbollah in the Middle East, or experiencing a Peruvian jail cell from the inside.

Traversing the arena of the world on foot, motorcycle, or even horseback, being on the road is the sole passion of his heart.

Getting himself into trouble at times, as a modern-day Marco Polo he follows in the footsteps of the first true explorers.

Do you wish to know where he sets his foot next?

www.ingramcontent.com/pod-product-compliance
Lightning Source LLC
Chambersburg PA
CBHW061739120626
46550CB00005B/1835